30

Short Walks Visiting Surrey Pubs

Daniel Somers

Illustrations
Jaqueline Hei

**MORNING MIST
PUBLICATIONS**

Published 1994

©Morning Mist Publications

ISBN 1 874476 06 3

Cover: The Volunteer, Sutton Abinger

Designed and Printed by
Advanced Data Graphics, Sevenoaks

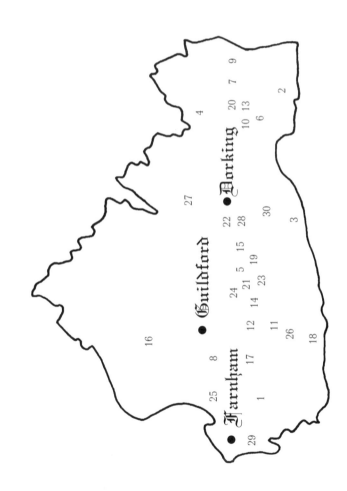

Surrey

16

25 8
Farnham
17
1
29

• Guildford
12
24 5 15
21 19
14 23
11
26
18

4

27
22 28
30
3

• Dorking
20 7 9
13
10 6
2

Index

$\mathfrak{Index}$ Cont.

21. 3.00
good

Introduction

Too often Surrey is viewed as a suburb of London. As this book, I hope, proves Surrey is in fact, a rural county of great beauty, blessed with a wide range of excellent pubs. In the book I have attempted to present a balance of the wildly differing Surrey countryside together with a varied selection of pubs which range from the traditional inn to the increasingly popular family style hostelry.

The two primary rules in selecting the walks are:-

    (a) Beautiful scenery

    (b) Real ale

Every pub featured serves real ale and these are the only beers I have listed at the end of each pub description.

This book is not intended for the walker who wants to clock up the miles. Instead, I recommend you keep to another rule - take your time, enjoy the scenery and above all enjoy the pubs!

Using This Guide

Choosing Your Walk and Pub

The walks are listed in order of distance (the shortest first), together with an "at a glance" guide to the ease of the walk. This guide is shown as a "Level" and is listed at the start of each walk as well as in the Index. There are three Levels:-

Level A - Easy. Short distance, mostly flat with easy route finding.

Level B - Moderate. One or two slopes with route finding generally very easy but extra care may be required.

Level C - Advanced. Slightly longer in distance but easy if you are reasonably fit. One or more steep climbs and some paths may be undefined.

Your confidence in route finding and general level of fitness will determine which walk you choose, though even the longest walk should be easily managed by the averagely fit adult.

A good description of each pub is given and to help, a simple key at the end of each description highlights the main features, such as separate restaurant, childrens' room, etc. I hope that eventually, you will have tried every pub, even if you do not attempt every walk!

Getting There, Parking and Route Finding

Most of the walks start from a parking area and meet the pub en route. A few start and finish at the pub, though you can of course, start and finish at every pub should you wish to do so. If you do, please only use the pub car park if you intend being a patron on the day. When roadside parking is the only option, please remember to be considerate to the local inhabitants. It is the responsibility of the individual to ensure that the car is parked safely, not obstructing access and most importantly, legally.

Although a sketch map is provided, I recommend you take an Ordnance Survey Landranger Map. The relevant map is listed at the beginning of each walk. Each starting point in addition to a description on how to get there, is given a grid reference point for quick location on the Landranger Map.

Nearly all the paths followed are marked on the Landranger Map and most are well trodden, so route finding should not be a problem. It is useful to familiarise yourself with the various path signs. The most obvious are the signs which actually say "footpath" or "bridleway" (a bridleway is a path open to cyclists and horse riders as well as people on foot), though much more common now are coloured arrows. Yellow denotes footpaths and blue, bridleways. A red arrow is a route open to all traffic. There is also a rapidly growing array of signs which designate specific walks such as long distance paths or nature trails. Where you follow these, I have included a description of the sign.

The routes are fairly simple and if you take your time (don't rush - even if it is near closing time!), study the map and directions carefully, you should complete your walk without mishap. If you do wander off the trail it is all the more important that you are carrying a Landranger Map, as it will not only help you find out where you went wrong, but also how you rejoin the walk.

Clothing

The English are always talking about the weather and for good reason. It is unreliable and unpredictable. For this reason, it is important to be sensibly dressed and prepared for any change. Take a small rucksack or an easy to carry bag and pack a jumper and waterproofs. Nine times out of ten you will probably not need them, but you will be thankful when you do. Many of the paths can be uneven and muddy so comfortable and sturdy footwear is sensible. Flipflops or high heels are definitely not recommended.

Pub Etiquette for Walkers

The fact that a pub is featured in this book is not a guarantee that you will be welcomed by the landlord, especially if you proceed to tread mud all over the carpet. Generally, walkers are welcome but this will only remain the case if they treat the pub with respect. To preserve a welcome for other walkers, please observe the following simple good manners.

- Only use the pub car park if you intend being a patron of the pub on the day.

- Unless the landlord gives permission, do not eat your own food on the pub premises. Not only is it rude, but you are probably missing out on some good pub grub.

- Do not wear your muddy boots in the bar. Instead leave them outside. The same goes for wet and muddy clothing.

- If you are walking as a group, telephone the pub in advance. This is both polite and practical, especially if you want to be assured of a hot meal.

- Do not assume children or dogs will be welcome. Where available, I have provided this information in the pub description but landlords and rules change. If in doubt, telephone first.

The Changing Countryside

Every walk and pub has been carefully researched and checked to ensure that the walks and pub descriptions are correct. Time however, does not stand still and changes may and probably will occur in the lifetime of this book. A new landlord can rapidly change a pub as can a new farmer the countryside. Although we have made every effort to ensure that the details in this book are correct, we accept no liability for errors, omissions or for any consequences arising from the use of this book. Any opinions on the pubs featured are purely those of the author.

The Country Code

Please ensure you follow The Country Code at all times (see inside front cover).

The Barley Mow
- Tilford Green

Courage. A picturesque pub overlooking a cricket green bordered on two sides by the River Wey. The pub has strong associations with cricket and the once famous cricketer Silver Billy Beldham was landlord here in the early 19th century. Today, cricket teams still take advantage of the pub's position to quench their thirst. The pub has changed little since Silver Billy's day and is all the better for it. You will find no noisy fruit machines or juke boxes, instead, the rapidly dying art of conversation is the order of the day. Simple but comfortable furniture graces the bar which, as you would expect, has it's fair share of cricket memorabilia. There are plenty of magazines available, should you not feel like conversing. The pub serves some good honest food which, in Summer, can be enjoyed in a garden that stretches down to the River Wey. The pub also opens a tea room in Summer, when apart from cricket for entertainment there is often a display of Morris Dancing.

   11.00am - 2.30pm, 6.00pm - 11.00pm
Sat - 11.30am - 3.00pm, 5.30pm - 11.00pm

Beers: Courage - Best Bitter, Directors;
John Smith - Bitter;
Wadsworth - 6X.

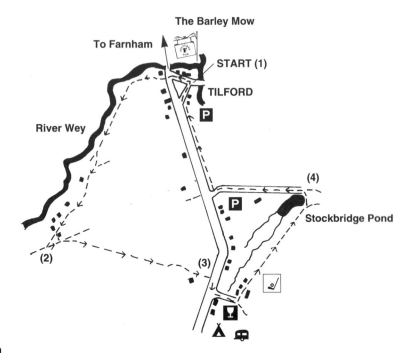

Terrain

Mostly flat along woodland paths. Can get muddy in places in wet weather.

Getting to the Start (Grid Ref. 874434)

The walk starts from Tilford Green where there is a small public car park. Tilford is found amongst a maze of lanes between the A3 and the A31. From the A3, follow the signs to Elstead and then follow the B3001 heading for Farnham, turning off when you see the first sign for Tilford. Thereon follow the Tilford signs until you arrive at the village green, reached by way of a small bridge over the River Wey. From the A31, drive to Farnham where you should join the B3001 signposted to Godalming. Thereafter, follow the signs to Tilford.

Tilford, apart from cricket, is famous for its famous oak tree and its two 13th century bridges, built by the monks of nearby Waverley Abbey. Sir J. M. Barrie based Never Never Land in his enchanting tale of Peter Pan on much of the surrounding countryside.

The walk

(1) Facing the pub, turn left to shortly arrive at a "T" junction at the other side of the green. On the way you will pass the famous Tilford Oak on your right which is behind a stone seat. Cross the road ahead to join a track at the other side and after passing through a gate fork left, turning immediately right to join a signposted footpath which runs between hedges. The path runs behind a nursery and then after passing through a gate, enters a wood. Follow the path through the wood with the River Wey on your right and when the path meets a track turn right, and immediately after, fork left to follow the main track passing a house on your right. Pass two more houses and then some outbuildings. After this follow a wide fenced path which continues to take you through the wood.

(2) On arriving at a wide track turn left and follow the track. Just after passing a gate on your left take a path which forks right, marked with a blue arrow. At first the path follows a fence to the right and after going over a crossing track follows a fence and a line of fields on your left. The path eventually meets the drive to a house on your right and here you should turn left and follow the drive to meet a road.

¾ mile

(3) Cross the road and join a tarmac drive the other side which runs alongside the Duke of Cambridge pub and signposted to Hankley Common Golf Club, as well as a caravan and camp site. On reaching the car park for the golf club turn left to go straight through the centre of the car park, pass to the left of a flagpole and join a track ahead which runs along the perimeter of the golf course. Eventually the track bends right, where you will see a pond (Stockbridge Pond) on your left. Leave the track at this point and take a narrow path which runs alongside the pond. On meeting a track at the far side of the pond, turn left, walking away from an Army training area sign.

1¼ miles

(4) Follow the track to its end where it meets a road. Do not join the road but turn right instead passing through a metal gate to take a track which runs parallel to the road. The track takes you back to the Green at Tilford, our starting point.

1¾ miles

2 miles

The Bell - Outwood

Free House. A lovely 17th century pub with a deserved reputation for excellent food. The pub itself is an attractive tile hung building with a large bell in a glass display case at the front. You are greeted as you enter by a wooden carving of the three monkeys, perhaps a subtle hint to your desired behaviour! Inside, the pub retains many of its original features, the carpeted lounge has two large fireplaces and an exposed beamed ceiling. Some interesting pictures adorn the walls and there is a display of some unusual objects from the past in the larger fireplace. Stretching towards the rear is the restaurant, which has such a good reputation that people travel for miles to eat here. Beer drinkers can choose from a wide and well chosen range of real ales which include up to five guest beers. If the general ambience, good beer and good food is not enough to attract you, the pub holds regular event nights which at the time of writing, include mystic evenings and Tudor nights. At the rear is a small garden where barbecues are held in Summer.

✕, ıOı, ⚶,  *All day.*

Beers: Charrington - IPA
                   Flowers - Original
                   Pilgrim - Progress
                   Guest Beers

Terrain

Very flat and easy walking through fields and woodland. The reason for the Level B grade is that the paths through the wood can be a little confusing and a good sense of direction helps.

Getting to the Start (Grid Ref. 327456)

The walk starts from Outwood village at the edge of the National Trust protected Outwood Common. The village, although remote, is easily reached from three main roads, the A25 at Bletchingley, the A23 at Salfords and the A22 at Blindley Heath. Follow the signs to the village and at the village green (easily identified by its 17th century windmill), take a gravel track opposite Gayhouse Lane (the lane which runs in front of the windmill). The track leads to a small parking area.

Outwood is famous for its windmill. Built in 1665, it is the oldest working windmill in England. Until 1960, there used to be two mills but the second collapsed in a storm.

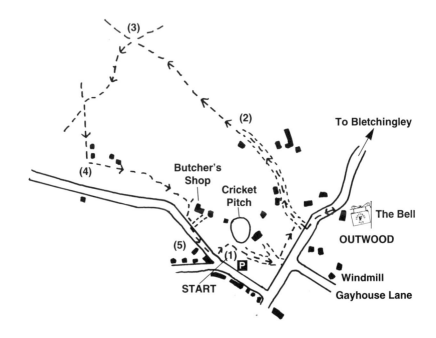

The Walk

(1) To start the walk, follow the gravel track from the car park back to the lane, where ahead you will see the old 17th century windmill. Do not join the lane but turn left across the green and on meeting another lane also marked as a Public Footpath, turn left. If you want to visit The Bell pub, cross this lane and continue straight ahead. You will soon see The Bell at the other side of a road on your right. Returning to our route, follow the lane past some cottages and then a small garage.

½ mile **(2)** When the lane ends beside a house on your left, continue straight ahead to shortly go into a field. Follow a prominent path across the field and on entering the next field, bear right to follow the field edge. If in doubt, follow the direction of the yellow footpath arrow.

¾ mile **(3)** At the far side of the field go over a stile and turn left along the edge of the next field. At the field corner, go over a stile and cross a small bridge to enter another field where you should continue ahead, keeping to the edge of the field. On your right Redhill is visible. At the far corner go over a stile and bear left to re-enter the wood at Outwood Common. After a short distance, the main path branches off to the right but you should maintain your route ahead. On meeting some cottages the path becomes a track and you should follow this as it bends left to arrive at a crossing track and small green.

1¼ miles **(4)** Go over the crossing track and at the other side take a grass path that forks gently right, passing Slate Cottage, before continuing through the woodland of Outwood Common. After 20 metres fork right maintaining your route ahead and after this keep to the path as it winds through the wood, at one point ignoring a narrow path off to the right. When the path forks, fork right and after a few paces, bear left to meet a "T" junction, another narrow path. Turn right to shortly reach a road.

1¾ miles **(5)** Turn left along the road passing the village butchers and just before you reach another road, Millers Lane, take a prominent path left, opposite the Old School House. When the village cricket pitch comes into view turn right and follow a track back to the car 2 miles park, our starting point.

The Punchbowl - Oakwoodhill (Okewoodhill)

Free House. An excellent village pub and once the local for that connoisseur of drink, Oliver Reed. Inside, a huge inglenook fire dominates an olde worlde bar and the floor consists of some of the largest flagstones I have seen. Casually comfortable, the solid pine furniture blends in well with the natural decor of the bar. Pass beneath the stairs and you will find a cosy restaurant which has an imaginative international menu. In the bar a large blackboard displays the daily specials. Outside, there is a small fenced seating area where, in Summer, you can enjoy the occasional barbecue. Across the road is the village cricket green where one can relax after all that hard eating and drinking.

✕, iOi, ⍭,  *All day.*

Beers: Badger - Best Bitter, Tanglefoot
Wadsworth - 6X
Guest Beer - changes regularly

Terrain

This is an easy walk which most people should complete without difficulty. One thing that may cause a problem are the woodland paths which are hidden by leaves in Autumn. This can cause difficulty in route finding and unless you have a good sense of direction, it may be better to avoid this walk in Autumn.

Getting to the Start (Grid Ref. 128381)

The walk starts from a deadend lane which leads to the village church. To get there, take the A29 to Ockley and at the southern end of the village, beside the village sign, take a narrow lane signposted to the Gatton Manor Hotel. At a "T" junction turn left, still following the signs for the hotel and keep to the lane for approximately ¾ mile until you see another narrow lane off to the left marked as a deadend and also by a somewhat weathered sign to the church. Take this to the church where parking is possible at the side of the lane (please do not park at the end of the lane, which is in fact a turning point).

The Walk

(1) To start, follow the lane to the church, go over a bridge and follow a tarmac path through the churchyard. *Oakwoodhill church is the most remote church in Surrey, built on the site of a Druid temple. The surrounding woodland was once renowned for its excellent hunting of wild boar.*

Pass in front of the church porch and immediately after, take a path left and exit the churchyard via a wooden gate. Thereafter, follow a wide path ahead through woodland, marked by a yellow footpath arrow. After a few paces, carry straight on (do not fork left), to soon bend right with the path, the path now running adjacent to a fence on your left. Sometime later, pass through a wooden rail and continue to follow a fenced path beside a field on your left. The path leads around the field with good views on your left of Leith Hill. Go over a stile and bear right along a track to shortly meet a road.

¼ mile **(2)** Turn left along the road taking care of the traffic and on meeting another road, turn left in the direction of the sign for Ockley and Dorking. After approximately 50 metres, you will arrive at The Punchbowl.

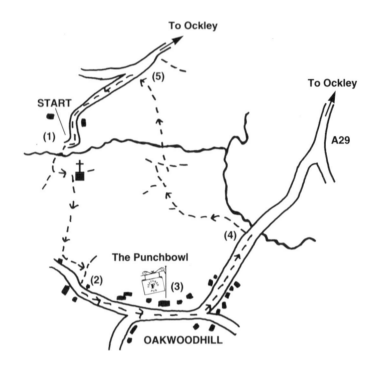

(3) From the pub, continue in the same direction as before along the road. Do not turn off, but follow the road as it bends left to go downhill. At the bottom of the hill, just before the road meets a bridge which crosses a narrow river, take a signposted public footpath left. This is opposite an Oakwoodhill sign.   ½ mile

(4) Follow a prominent path through a wood and later, on meeting a fork, fork right. Soon after, the path bends left and immediately after this, you should take a narrow path right. As a guide, after about 15 metres, this path crosses a tiny winding stream before proceeding to wind through woodland. You will soon meet a crossing path in front of a wooden post marked with yellow arrows. Turn right here and after 30 paces at a "T" junction beside another wooden post with footpath arrows, turn left to follow a wider path through the wood. Go over a bridge across a stream and follow the path uphill to soon run alongside a field on your right.   ¾ mile

(5) On meeting a lane, turn left and then left again onto the lane which leads to Oakwood church. Follow this back to the church and our starting point.   1½ miles

2 miles

𝕽amblers 𝕽est
- 𝕮hipstead

Free House. Until recently this lovely rambling half timbered 14th century building was an exclusive restaurant called Dene Farm. The building was originally part of a farm. Dene is Saxon for a hollow or storage area, which would indicate a barn or something similar stood here prior to the existing building. A clever refurbishment has created a popular family style pub. There are several drinking areas with the main bar being panelled and a separate restaurant. The interior decorators have kept a number of cosy corners and the wide range of tables cater for large groups or the intimate couple. Blackboards are displayed on the walls announcing 'specials' and on one is an "Ode To A Rambler" which is most appropriate. There is a large beer garden at the rear. Both the restaurant and bar menus are extensive, offering a remarkably wide and original selection of food, probably a welcome hangover from its restaurant days. The proprietors have not ignored their beer, and with no less than eight real ales available, the pub offers one of the best selection of beer in the area.

 *All day.*

Beers: Fullers - London Pride
Morland - Old Speckled Hen
Whitbread - Flowers Original, Strong Country, Fremlins
Guest Beer

Terrain
Well used paths along the edge of a steep sided valley with one fairly
steep descent to reach the pub. A good walk to start with.

Getting to the Start (Grid Ref. 273583)
The walk starts from the public car park at the bottom of Chipstead
Valley on the B2219, the car park is marked on the Ordnance Survey
Map. The B2219 can be reached from Banstead Village or from the
B2032 which runs between Coulsdon and the A217 Tadworth
roundabout. If you do not have a car, then Chipstead Railway Station
is only a few minutes walk from the car park. There is a public
convenience and a cafe at the car park.

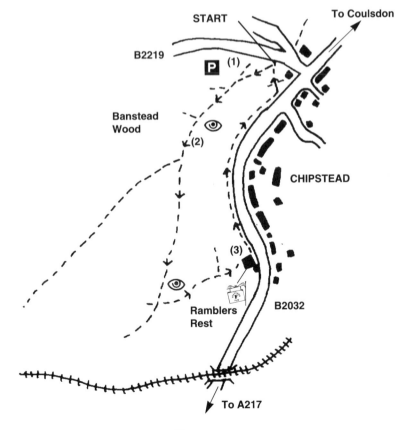

The Walk

(1) From the car park, facing away from the road, leave by the exit at the top left hand corner to follow a prominent path that leads gently uphill. When you reach a "T" junction in front of a fence, turn left and continue to progress uphill keeping the fence on your right, do not be tempted to take one of the paths on the right leading into the wood. There are some good views to your left over Chipstead Valley before the path you are on also disappears into the wood. *One famous resident of Chipstead was Sir Edward Banks who specialised in building bridges. His two most famous works are London and Waterloo Bridges.*

¼ mile **(2)** After passing a small gate on your right the path levels out and there is a bench on which you can rest. At a fork keep left on the more prominent path to shortly come out onto open hillside, where below to your left you can see the Ramblers Rest, our featured pub. Maintain your route ignoring any turnings off to the left or right, to later follow the lefthand edge of a field and continue until you reach a crossing track. Turn left onto the track to start our descent to the pub, ignoring a path off to the left immediately after joining. Stay on the track to eventually arrive at the Ramblers Rest pub.

1¼ miles **(3)** From the pub facing a road (the B2032) turn left along the pavement and after a short distance pass through a wooden gate and maintain your route ahead along a narrow path. When the path ends opposite Hazelwood Lane, turn left going uphill, away from the road, passing to the left of a bench and a few paces after this on meeting a crossing path, turn right and follow it back to
2 miles the car park.

𝕿𝖍𝖊 𝖁𝖔𝖑𝖚𝖓𝖙𝖊𝖊𝖗 - 𝕾𝖚𝖙𝖙𝖔𝖓 𝕬𝖇𝖎𝖓𝖌𝖊𝖗

Friary Meux. The Volunteer, situated on the side of the Tillingbourne valley, must have one of the prettiest locations of any pub in Surrey. The long single bar was once three separate rooms. Cleverly, all three fireplaces still remain, which make the pub a cosy retreat in Winter. A third of the bar (the first room) has a tiled floor, the other two bare floorboards covered with large rugs. On the walls military pictures dominate. The furniture is a mixture of old and reproduction, amongst which are some lovely old carved benches. To the rear of the pub is a separate restaurant which serves some ambitious food. Good traditional pub grub is available in the bar. Outside, there is a delightful terraced garden built into the valley side, a lovely place to spend a Summer lunchtime. If you cannot bear to leave, the pub does Bed and Breakfast.

  11.00am-3.00pm, 6.00pm-11.00pm

Beers: Friary Meux - Best Bitter
Ind Coope - Burton Ale
Guest Beers

Terrain

The going is fairly easy throughout except for one steep descent to reach the pub. The type of paths followed can be equally divided into woodland, field and lane. The last stretch (lane) is a slow, steady ascent which can be tiring after a drink at The Volunteer.

Getting to the Start (Grid Ref. 105450)

The walk starts from a small parking area beside Holmbury St. Mary Youth Hostel (marked by a red triangle on the Ordnance Survey Map). The car park is reached by taking the B2126 where in between Sutton Abinger and Holmbury St. Mary, you should turn onto a narrow lane which is signposted to the Youth Hostel. Follow the lane to its end to find the parking area.

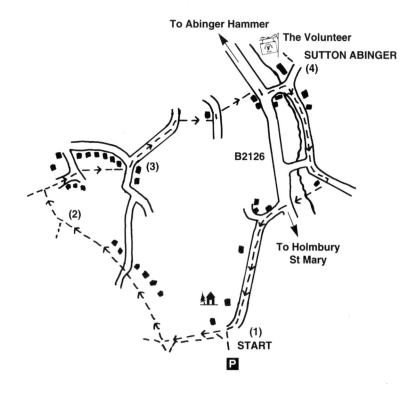

The Walk

(1) From the car park facing a Hurtwood Control sign, turn right. Follow the wide path through the Hurtwood and after a short distance fork right and then right again passing a gate on your right. Do not be tempted to join the sunken track on your left at this point. After a short distance, the path forks again and this time you can take either path as they re-join shortly. You will soon pass another gate on your right, after which the path runs alongside a field on the same side and then descends the side of a valley. It later passes behind some houses and then across a tarmac drive, where you should follow the path ahead the other side.

(2) Go over a stile, continue ahead along the edge of the field and after a short distance, fork right following a narrow path across the centre of the field. At the far side of the field, bear right. Follow the path uphill between a garden on your right and a field on your left. This leads onto a tarmac drive which you should follow ahead. When the drive bends left (approximately 10 metres) continue ahead and follow a narrow path which runs behind gardens.
½ mile

(3) The path leads to a lane onto which you should turn left (do not turn left again on to another lane). to descend gently between fields. As the lane bends left, you will see a signposted Public Footpath on your right. Take this to soon reach another lane. Turn left along the lane and after approximately 30 paces, turn right opposite the entrance to Stile Cottage, to join a fenced path between fields. As the path goes over the brow of the hill you will enjoy some lovely views ahead of The Volunteer pub. On meeting a road, the B2126, turn right and then left into Raikes Lane to arrive at The Volunteer.
¾ miles

(4) From The Volunteer, take the road opposite the pub, passing the entrance to Water Lane House. Soon after passing a narrow lane off to your right, turn right on to a narrow path which runs alongside the perimeter fencing of a house on your right, Griffins. As a guide, the path starts beside a NO HORSES sign. Go over a stile and follow a prominent path across a field going over a stream at its centre. At the far side of the field cross the B2126 and join a lane the other side which leads to the Youth Hostel. Fork left and follow the signs to the Youth Hostel to reach the car park, our starting point.
1¼ miles

2 miles

Nearby Attractions

Abinger Hammer. An attractive village with unusual clock
Leith Hill, N.T. The highest point in South East England

The Plough
- Leigh

King & Barnes. A beautiful 15th century weather-boarded pub overlooking the village green. A Victorian extension houses the public bar which although basic, is extremely comfortable. The narrow lounge in the oldest part of the pub has one of the lowest beams I have ever had the misfortune to bump into! Thankfully, it is well padded to avoid injury. At the far end of the lounge is a small restaurant. The food is locally renowned and justifiably so. Regular specials compliment the regular favourites. There is plenty of seating outside to take advantage of those balmy Summer evenings.

✗, ⅰΟⅼ, ᚠ, **OPEN** *11.00am-2.30pm, 6.00pm-11.00pm*

Beers: King & Barnes - Sussex Bitter, Broadwood, Festive, Christmas Ale

Terrain

Flat with most of the walk through fields. At points you meet and follow the River Mole and in wet weather the going here can be very muddy.

Getting to the Start (Grid Ref. 224469)

The walk starts from the centre of Leigh village in front of The Plough pub. Leigh is well signposted from the A25 and A217 near Reigate. Parking is possible around the village green and opposite the church but please be considerate of the local residents.

The green still with the old village pump, rambling houses, weatherboarded pub and church is the prettiest part of the village. The name Leigh is pronounced locally as "lie".

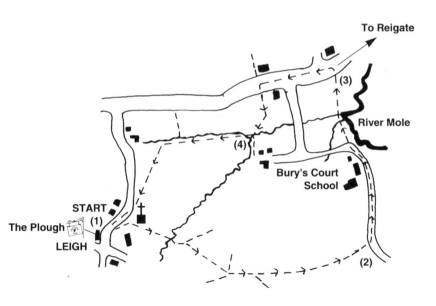

The Walk

(1) To start, with your back to The Plough, cross the road, bear left across the village green and take a signposted footpath through the churchyard. Pass to the right of the church and thereafter, follow a prominent footpath ahead, at the end of which you should go over a stile into a field. Go straight across the field bearing slightly diagonally right and at the far side, cross a bridge into another field. Bear left and after a few paces, go over a stile on your left into yet another field where you should turn immediately right to follow the field edge. On reaching the field corner, go over a stile on your right and then turn left to follow a fenced bridleway. This soon ends in front of two gates. Pass through the left hand gate, the smaller of the two, and continue ahead along the left hand edge of a field. At the far side, pass through another gate and follow a prominent path ahead into Bell Copse. As you continue through the copse, the path widens into a track and continues thereafter, between fields to reach a semi-tarmacced drive.

1 mile **(2)** Turn left to follow the drive which belongs to Bury's Court School and keep to the drive to soon pass the school buildings. Just after passing Keeper's Cottage, go over a stile on your right into a field and cross the field, following the course of the River Mole on your right. The River Mole is so called because at certain points it has been known to disappear underground, re-appearing further along its course. Cross a stream and then a second stream via a wooden footbridge and after this, carry straight on across the field, heading for a house at the far side.

1½miles **(3)** Go over a stile onto a road and turn left to follow the road passing the entrance to Bury's Court School. Soon after this, join a footpath on your left opposite a post box, which runs along the side of a field and then bears diagonally right to cross it. At the other side, go over a footbridge and turn right to follow the bank of a stream. After about 20 metres, go over another footbridge on your right, crossing the stream once more and then follow the path ahead along the edge of a field.

1¾ miles **(4)** After the field, the path continues in the same direction along the edge of two more fields. In the third field, ignore a stile and marked footpath on your right and continue ahead to enter a fourth field where you should go diagonally left across the centre, heading for the church at Leigh. At the far side, leave the field and turn left along a lane to reach the village green at Leigh, our
2¼ miles starting point.

𝕿𝖍𝖊 𝕻𝖗𝖎𝖓𝖈𝖊 𝕬𝖑𝖇𝖊𝖗𝖙 - 𝕭𝖑𝖊𝖙𝖈𝖍𝖎𝖓𝖌𝖑𝖊𝖞

Friary Meux. The pub is one of several attractive tile hung buildings which line the main village street. This building dates from the 15th century and the number of exposed beams are evidence of the builders' skill. There are two cosy bars and a separate slender restaurant, cleverly designed for intimacy whilst making full use of the limited space. The extensive a la carte menu changes regularly, a testament to the chef's professionalism as is the excellent quality of the food. The pub walls are decorated by pictures of vintage cars and engine parts (cleaned) replace the traditional brass ornaments. At the rear is a lovely well cared for garden which, in Summer, is a delight to relax in.

✕, ℐ𝒪ℐ, ℸ, 𝗢𝗣𝗘𝗡 *11.00am-3.00pm, 6.00pm-11.00pm*

Beers: Friary Meux - Best Bitter
Inde Coope - Burton Ale
Youngs - Special, Winter Warmer

Terrain
Gentle sloping fields with a small amount of lane walking. Good views.

Getting to the Start (Grid Ref. 327507)
The walk starts from the War Memorial beside the Post Office at
Bletchingley High Street. Bletchingley is easily reached as its High
Street is also the A25. The village is situated between Redhill and
Godstone, both of which have connections with the M25. Parking is
possible in Bletchingley's wide High Street.

*Bletchingley was once dominated by a large castle, destroyed during a
battle in 1264. At that time the village was a market town which is
why it has such a wide High Street. The Whyte Harte Hotel used to be
the site of the village Parliamentary elections, before the Reform Bill
in 1832 did away with the notorious Rotton Boroughs.*

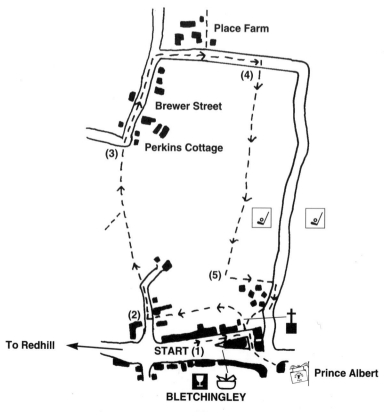

The Walk

(1) From the War Memorial follow the pavement behind the Post Office and in front of a small shop, Kiddies Catwalk, once the old butchers, and at the end turn left into the churchyard. Take the tarmac path which leads round the left of the church, then leave the churchyard to follow a tarmac path between gardens. Do not turn off but continue until you eventually meet a narrow lane in front of a set of steps.

(2) Turn right along the lane and later when it bends right into Dormers Farm, leave it to take a narrow path ahead which goes downhill. Stay on the path until you eventually meet a track and follow the track ahead to arrive at a lane beside Perkins Cottage.

¼ miles

(3) Follow the lane ahead which passes through the pleasant hamlet of Brewer Street, where one of the more interesting buildings is the lovely Brewer Street Farm. This is a half timbered building which was once the gatehouse to a grand medieval palace. The palace was once home to Anne of Cleves. Shortly after the farm turn right onto another lane signposted to Bletchingley and Godstone and after passing a pond on your right, turn right onto a signposted footpath into a field.

¾ miles

(4) Go straight across the field heading for Bletchingley church, visible ahead. At the far side go over a stile and maintain your route to cross three successive fields. At the end of the third field go over a stile, up a bank onto a golf course and here bear right along the edge of the golf course, still heading for Bletchingley church.

1¼ miles

(5) On reaching a corner of the golf course, go over a stile and turn left. At a lane in front of the entrance to Bletchingley Golf Club, turn right. Follow the lane uphill to later re-enter the churchyard and fork left, thereby walking left round the church. Exit when you meet the brick path and then turn left to come out at the High Street beside a Rolls Royce garage. The Prince Albert is on your left on the other side of the road. To get back to our starting point, turn right along the High Street and you will soon see the War Memorial.

1¾ miles

2¼ miles

Nearby Attractions
Godstone Village
Godstone Farm - Godstone.

The Withies Inn
- Compton

Free House. An attractive 16th century building surrounded by one of the best pub gardens I have ever had the pleasure to drink in. The garden is a hint of what is to come. Step over the threshold and you are greeted by a luxurious interior, dominated by a richly carved oak bar. The warm discrete lighting, solid beams, antique furniture and huge inglenook fire can give the illusion that you are enjoying a drink in another century. There is a separate restaurant that serves excellent individual cuisine and, apart from the beer, for many this is the main reason to visit. You are also welcome to enjoy a meal in the bar.

 *10.30am-3.00pm, 6.00pm-11.00pm*

Beers: King & Barnes - Sussex Bitter
         Tetley - Bitter
         Guest Beers

Terrain

Mainly gentle sloping fields with, in places, some fine views of the Hogs Back. A small amount of road walking.

Getting to the Start (Grid Ref. 963467)

The walk starts from the pub. To get there take the B3000 between the A3 and A3100 where there is a Withies Inn signpost at the beginning of the lane that leads to the pub. Roadside parking is possible (please be considerate) near the pub. Please only use the pub car park if you intend patronising the pub on the day.

Compton is an attractive village with many fine half timbered buildings. It has an interesting church which is unique in that it is the only two storeyed sanctuary in England.

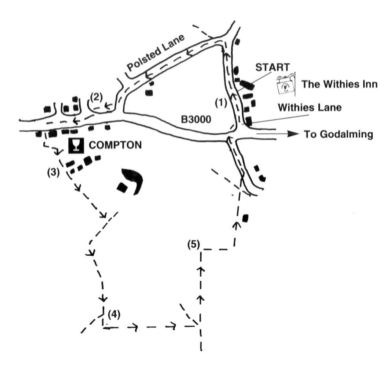

The Walk

(1) Facing the pub, turn left and follow the lane and keep to it as it later bends left, ignoring a dead end lane off to your right. Continue past a small housing estate on your right to meet a green on the same side. Turn right and cut across the green to reach the B3000.

¼ mile **(2)** Turn right along the main road until you arrive opposite another pub, The Harrow, where you should cross the road opposite its car park. Walk through the car park to join a signposted public footpath which takes the form of a track running gently downhill between houses. The track soon ends and continues in the form of a narrow path which bends left to run behind some houses. After crossing a stile the path continues between fields.

¾ mile **(3)** The path then leads behind Field Place Farm where you need to cross a series of three stiles and continue in the same direction. Walk straight across a field to a stile the other side. The stile as a guide, is on the left hand perimeter of the field and to your right is an area of woodland. Once over the stile you will arrive at a track on to which you should turn right going gently uphill. The track descends to follow the right hand perimeter of a field, with the woods still on your right. Note: The footpath from here officially runs to the right of the field behind a fence, but as this is often overgrown, many people walk within the field along its perimeter. If you do this, it will be necessary to leave the field near the far corner to re-join the official route.

1¼ miles **(4)** When the path nears the far side of the field, go through a kissing gate, ignoring a bridleway off to your right, to follow the field perimeter round. At the next field corner ignore steps off to your right going uphill and bear left, to continue following the field perimeter round. Do not go over the stile into the field on your left but keep to the perimeter path at all times.

1½ miles **(5)** Some time later the path naturally twists right to follow the righthand perimeter of another field. At the field corner beside a white farm gate on your right, turn left to follow a track along the edge of the same field. After approximately 50 metres look out for a narrow path on your right marked by a blue bridleway arrow which you should take to continue ahead. The path soon rejoins the track after which you should turn right and follow it to reach a lane. Turn left along the lane to reach the B3000. Cross the road to 2¼ miles join Withies Lane and follow the sign to the pub, The Withies Inn.

Nearby Attractions

Loseley House. An historic country house now famous for its ice-cream.

The Watts Gallery & Memorial Chapel. Situated West of Compton village. The Chapel, built in the shape of a Greek cross was erected by the painter's widow.

𝕿𝖍𝖊 𝕮𝖆𝖗𝖕𝖊𝖓𝖙𝖊𝖗𝖘 𝕬𝖗𝖒𝖘 - 𝕷𝖎𝖒𝖕𝖘𝖋𝖎𝖊𝖑𝖉 𝕮𝖍𝖆𝖗𝖙

Friary Meux. A very local pub which overlooks a large green, part of Limpsfield Chart, a large expanse of common protected by the National Trust. The large single bar has a segregated restaurant which serves good basic pub food including a roast on Sundays. The portions should keep you going for days. The bar is carpeted and has recently been refurbished in the traditional style, outside there is a small garden. Please note, children under 14 and dogs are not allowed in the bar.

🍴, ⚏. 🪧 *11.00am-3.00pm, 6.00pm-11.00pm*

Beers: Friary Meux - Best Bitter
            Tetley - Bitter
            Ind Coope - Burton Ale

Terrain

An energetic walk which explores the Greensand Ridge. From the Chart, after a small amount of lane walking, the route descends the ridge through fields with fine views South across The Weald. After more attractive lane walking, you then climb the ridge which can be tough going if you are unfit, and at the top follow a roadside path back to the pub.

Getting to the Start (Grid Ref. 426518)

The walk starts from the green in front of the Carpenters Arms. There is a small parking area opposite The Mill House, a house to the right of the pub at the end of the lane. Roadside parking is also possible in front of the pub. The green and pub is just off the B269 between the A25 at Oxted and Crockham Hill, North of Edenbridge. The biggest landmark on the green is the village church, St. Andrews. On seeing the church, take the road that passes in front of it, and you will soon see the Carpenters Arms on the left.

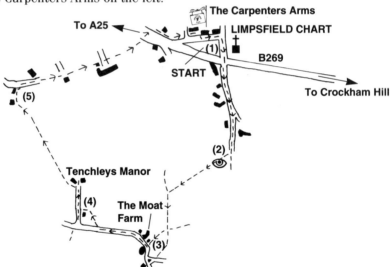

The Walk

(1) From the green walk along the road which passes in front of the church to reach and cross the B269. At the other side follow a narrow lane, Trevereux Hill, also signposted as a Public Bridleway. Keep to the lane admiring some of the lovely properties you pass, and particularly the old school which still has a bell tower although is now minus the bell. Do not take the turning left signposted to a number of properties and also as a Public Footpath, but keep to the tarmac lane going downhill. Shortly after this take a signposted Public Footpath on your right along a grass track to enter a field. Please note, if you continue along the lane until the tarmac runs out you know you have gone too far and missed the turning right.

½ mile   **(2)** From the top of the hill you have particularly good views across the Surrey Weald. Go diagonally right across the field and at the far

26

corner go through a gate to follow a narrow path along the edge of a strip of woodland. On entering a field, maintain your route by keeping to the field edge and following a strip of woodland on your left. About two thirds of the way across the field go over a stile on your left and follow the edge of another field. At the far side go over a stile ahead into another field and cross it by going diagonally right downhill to reach a lane.

(3) Turn right along the lane passing between a pond and beautiful 16th century farmhouse. Keep to the lane as it bends left in front of some cottages and continue until you see a signposted Public Footpath on your right. Take the footpath to enter a field. Go diagonally left across the field and leave the field by going over a small bridge. Cross a small grass area to shortly reach a drive (the original road from Limpsfield to Edenbridge). `1 mile`

(4) Turn right along the drive and as you approach Tenchleys Manor Farm, turn left onto another track which runs alongside the farm buildings. At the end of the track, go over a stile into a field and continue to follow the edge of the field. When this bends left, maintain your direction across the field going uphill. At the far side go over a stile to follow a sunken path uphill. The path later runs behind some gardens and then bends right to meet a track. `1½ miles`

(5) Turn right onto the track and after passing a couple of houses continue ahead along a path to shortly arrive beside a cottage, The Hollies. Maintain your route ahead (do not join the drive) following a prominent path through woodland, also part of the ancient common, Limpsfield Chart. Cross a tarmac drive and shortly after the B269, and at the other side turn right along the pavement which is also marked as a Public Footpath - Note Saltbox House on your right which literally used to be used to store salt brought from the coast for London. Later, cross a side road and follow a track the other side, past a number of houses and at "T" junction, turn right and immediately fork left to arrive at the lane beside the Carpenters Arms. `2 miles` `2½ miles`

Nearby Attractions
Titsey Park. A private park with restricted public access allowing fine walks.
Chartwell N.T., Home of Winston Churchill.
Toys Hill and Ide Hill N.T. Two hills of traditional heath and woodland affording good views across The Weald to the South Downs.
Squerryes Court - Westerham. Large house with some fine tapestries and period furniture, set in magnificent grounds.
Quebec House N.T. - Westerham. 17th century house once home to General Wolfe

The Dolphin
- Betchworth

Youngs. The Dolphin, up until 1926, used to brew its own beer. It now serves in my opinion some of the best kept beer in Surrey and compliments it with good traditional pub food. The front bar area has a couple of solid wooden tables which sit comfortably on a flagstone floor. On one side is large inglenook fire, a blessing in Winter, and the whole scene is overlooked by a large picture of HRH The Queen Mother. On the reverse side of the inglenook is another small bar and stretching towards the rear is a lounge area where most people tend to eat. The lack of electronic machines helps to retain the traditional character of the pub.

 *11.00am-3.00pm, 5.30pm-11.00pm*

Beers: Youngs – Bitter, Winter Warmer.

Terrain

A very easy and pleasant walk mostly along the banks of the River Mole. In wet weather the land close to the river tends to flood so choose your day out with care.

Getting to the Start (Grid Ref. 198496)

The walk starts from the village green at Brockham. Brockham is easily reached and well signposted from the A25, just east of Dorking.

Brockham is a classic Surrey village with an assortment of period houses and a church overlooking a large green. W.G. Grace used to play cricket on the green though it is now more famous for staging the largest Guy Fawkes bonfire in Surrey. On the North side of the green sits Surrey's oldest Chapel.

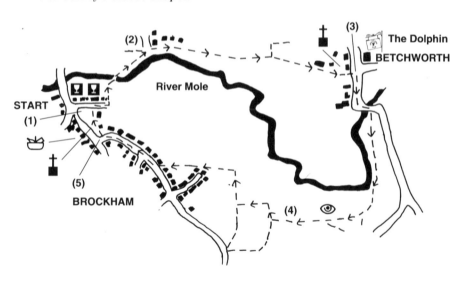

The walk starts from the green at Brockham village, where parking is available around the green. There are two pubs here, The Royal Oak and The Duke's Head, both Friary Meux.

(1) To start the walk, from Brockham green, follow the lane past The Duke's Head and when it meets the entrance to Brockham Court Farm, follow a tarmac path left signposted as a public bridleway. After crossing the river Mole, turn right along a track in the direction of a blue "GW" arrow, which from here guides your way to the Dolphin Pub at Betchworth.

¼ mile **(2)** to reach The Dolphin, follow the track until it meets a house ahead and fork right to follow a path running above the river Mole. This runs behind houses and then continues between fields where, at the end of the second field you should pass another path off to the left and carry straight on. A short while on, go over a concrete farm track to soon arrive at another drive behind Betchworth church. Walk through the churchyard and exit via a stone gateway the other side to arrive at a road in front of The Dolphin pub.

Betchworth was once dominated by a castle but this disappeared during the reign of Queen Anne. The village is unique as in the past no less than three of its inhabitants have been medical advisors to the Royal family.

1 mile **(3)** Turn right to follow the road and after passing over the river Mole a second time, take a signposted footpath right which leads across a field. At the far side of the field, go over a stile and follow a path uphill to enter another field. Bear right to follow the edge of the field and on meeting a large oak tree (and when the edge of the field bends right leading down to the river Mole), continue straight ahead along the edge of a ridge. You will at the same time, enjoy lovely views right over the river.

1¾ miles **(4)** At the far side of the field, go over a stile and follow a fenced path which skirts another field. When the path arrives at a "T" junction turn right along a path which follows the edge of a field and then bends left to run between fields. At the far side, it reaches another "T" junction. Turn right and follow the path back to Brockham where on meeting a road, you should turn right to head for and reach the church.

2½ miles **(5)** Take a tarmac path to the right of the church to arrive at the village green, our starting point.

Nearby Attractions
Denbies Vineyard - Dorking. The largest vineyard in England with a visitors centre and shop.

Box Hill N.T. - Dorking. Prominent hill on the North Downs, famous for its views.

The White Horse
- Hascombe

Friary Meux. This is a superb traditional pub which has managed to add popular attractions such as a conservatory and restaurant without diminishing the character which has taken centuries to build. The pub is made up of a number of small rooms, all with their own identity. The bar has a wooden floor and is furnished with long pine benches and a pleasant assortment of additional furniture, including a barrel which has been cut in half to form a couple of seats. The beamed ceiling is covered with dried hops and to complete the traditional scene, there is a warming wood burning stove. The lounge which is carpeted, has two rooms, one of which opens out to the conservatory. The restaurant, with the original brick floor, is a long room to the rear of the pub tastefully decorated allowing diners to enjoy their meal in plush and cosy surroundings, whilst retaining the olde worlde feel of a traditional pub. The food is excellent, especially the puddings. In Summer the pub is famous for its barbecues which are held in the large garden on the lower slopes of Hascombe Hill.

Beers: Adnams - Southwold Bitter
Friary Meux - Best Bitter
Marston - Pedigree

Terrain

The walk explores the wooded Hascombe Hill from where there are glorious views in virtually every direction of the compass. Apart from a long steady ascent at the beginning, the going is fairly easy. There are a number of minor crossing paths so care is needed in places.

Getting to the Start (Grid Ref.002397)

The walk starts from in front of the White Horse Pub at Hascombe. The pub and Hascombe are on the B2130 south of Godalming. There is limited street parking but it is possible to park on the grass verge opposite the pub. Please, only use the pub car park if you intend patronising the pub on the day.

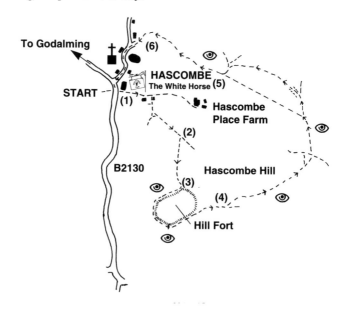

The Walk

(1) To start, take the tarmac drive to the right of the pub and when the tarmac ends turn right onto the gravel drive to Hascombe Place Farmhouse. Take a narrow path that runs along the righthand side of a wooden garage and go over a stile to follow a signposted public footpath which leads gently uphill between banks. At a junction of paths fork left to, after a short distance, join a track where you should continue ahead, maintaining your progress uphill.

(2) Further on take a prominent path that forks right thereby leaving the track (make sure you don't miss it). The path runs along the edge of the hill passing through a forest of rhododendron bushes. At the top you will arrive at a "T" junction which is also marked by some particularly high beech trees. Ahead is a bank, all that remains of the ramparts of an Iron Age hill fort. *The hill, 644 ft. in height, is the highest in the area and without trees, would have commanded valuable views to the fort's defenders. In the 19th century, the hill was used as a telegraph station.* ¼ mile

(3) Turn right and continue following the path along the edge of the hill with the bank of the fort on your left. The path continues to follow the edge of the hill affording views at first to the north, then west and finally south. ½ mile

(4) Eventually the path forks and you should take the lefthand fork, the higher path, continuing to skirt the top of the hill. Quite some distance later the path begins to descend through a beech wood and on reaching the corner of a field on your left, forks right to soon arrive at a crossing track. Go over the crossing track and take a prominent path the other side. You are now truly spoilt with lovely views both to your left and right. When the path later forks, take the lefthand fork passing between some wooden posts, keeping to the more prominent path. ¾ mile

(5) Much later a path joins from your right. At the same time the trees give way to allow lovely views to the east and to the north over a peaceful valley that runs down into Hascombe. Do not turn right but maintain your route ahead. The path now descends and eventually arrives at Hascombe Village. Hascombe is a picturebook village encircling a large pond, complete with resident ducks. The small village church, despite its appearance, was only built in 1863 and is a good example of how the Victorians recreated an earlier style of building. 1¾ miles

(6) Follow the lane ahead to skirt Hascombe village pond. After passing the church the lane leads back to the B2130 and the White Horse pub, our starting point. 2¼ miles

Nearby Attractions

Winkworth Arboretum N.T. A beautiful landscaped hillside of many rare trees and shrubs overlooking two lakes. There is a small gift shop and tea room at the car park on the B2130.

The Ram Cider House
- Catteshall

Free House. As you approach this unusual pub, you instantly know you are in for a treat. This lovely 16th century wattle and daub cottage would grace any fairytale with the magic continuing inside. The pub consists of two tiny bars and only slightly larger lounge. The bar has just four tables (two pushed together) and in one wall is a large fireplace with two benches where you can sit and still with its original oven door. One of the walls has a glass display panel allowing you to view the original wattle and daub. The lounge is slightly more plush with the emphasis on preserving the character of the building. A third small room (the public bar) has just enough room for a darts board. At the rear is a lovely large garden which has a ram carved out of a log, though the pub's name is derived from a ram pump which is still standing (used to pump water up the hill) and not the animal. There is a good range of food on offer with the menu changing regularly. When I last visited, I enjoyed their 'tipsy beef stew' which was delicious. No real ales are on offer, instead cider is the order of the day of which there is a huge variety, the main ones being listed below.

 *11.00am-2.30pm. 6.00pm-11.00pm*

Cider: Bulmers - Medium, Dry
                Symonds - Scrumpy Jack

Terrain

Flat. A little road walking with the rest along fenced paths and finally the tow path. Being close to water the going can obviously become muddy.

Getting to the Start (Grid Ref. 980447)

The walk starts from the public car park (Pay and Display) on the A3100 at Farncombe. The car park is beside The Leathern Bottle pub and opposite Catteshall Road.

The Walk

(1) To start the walk, from the car park cross the A3100 and follow Catteshall Road the other side. Follow the road over the canal, past The Boathouse "where you can get a cup of tea" and continue past a small housing estate to eventually turn left on to Catteshall Lane. After a short distance you will arrive at The Ram House.

Catteshall incidentally, is an ancient name and means 'hill of the wild cat'. Is it just coincidence that recent sightings of the so-called 'Surrey puma', a huge wild cat, have been on the wooded

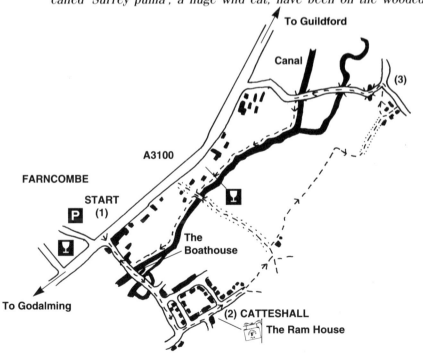

35

slopes above the pub?

(2) Fork left in front of the pub and follow the road to its end beside a small cul-de-sac. Continue ahead along a track and after a short distance, fork left thereby maintaining your route ahead. On reaching a crossing track turn left in the direction of a footpath sign, then after a few paces turn right to go down a driveway to a house. Pass to the left of the house then bear left to join a narrow fenced path which passes to the left of some outbuildings. The path then runs between fields with views to your left of the canal. Eventually it bends right, and soon after bends left on to a track. Follow the track until you see a stile on your left beside a brick wall. Go over the stile and follow a fenced path between gardens, to shortly go over another stile into a field. Go diagonally right across the field and at the far side go over a stile onto a lane.

(3) Turn left along the lane to shortly meet a second lane and turn left again to follow this lane over a couple of bridges crossing the River Wey and continue to soon reach a third bridge which goes over the canal. Go over the bridge and turn left to follow the tow path all the way back to the bridge beside The Boathouse. Turn right along the lane and retrace your steps to the car park, our starting point.

Nearby Attractions

Godalming. Historic town with an unusual Town Hall and many attractive side streets. Godalming was the first town in the world to have electric street lighting.

Loseley House. An historic country house, now famous for its ice-cream.

𝔖𝔨𝔦𝔪𝔪𝔦𝔫𝔤𝔱𝔬𝔫 ℭ𝔞𝔰𝔱𝔩𝔢 - 𝔕𝔢𝔦𝔤𝔞𝔱𝔢 ℌ𝔢𝔞𝔱𝔥

Friary Meux. One of the best preserved pubs in Surrey, probably because of its position which is at the end of a rough track (Bonnys Road) on Reigate Heath. The pub consists of four very different rooms. The front bar, a relatively modern extension has some lovely large windows which allow views to the North Downs. The loosely matched furniture would grace any antique shop and if you are not happy just to mellow, there is an unusual version of hoopla involving a horn. The rear bar, the most cosy, has a huge inglenook fire, doors to the gent's toilets leading off to one side are marked 'Tool Shed' and 'Potting Shed'. The serving bar is something of a museum, from the ceiling hangs an impressive collection of pipes and a skull, perhaps a subtle hint to the dangers of smoking. On one side is an Olympic torch from the 14th Olympics, a number of stuffed animals complete the scene. The food is a range of basic but hearty basket meals. Outside there is seating at the front and side of the pub, but you will be missing a unique experience if you do not go inside.

 11.00am-2.30pm, 5.30pm-11.00pm

Beers: Flowers - IPA
Friary Meux - Best Bitter
Greene King - IPA, Abbot Ale

Terrain

A gentle walk through some lovely heathland and farm fields. Much of the walk follows the banks of the River Mole where it can be very muddy in wet weather and, in extreme conditions, can even flood. Choose your day out with care.

Getting to the Start (Grid Ref. 239503)

The walk starts from the car park (marked on the Ordnance Survey Map) at Reigate Heath. Unless you are familiar with the area the simplest way to get there is via the A25, just west of Reigate. Take the turning south, beside the Black Horse pub and shortly after passing the last of the cottages on your left you will see parking areas either side of the road. The walk starts from the parking area on your right.

The Walk

(1) To start, from the car park pass through some wooden rails at the southern end (the end furthest from the A25) to join a sandy track, well used by horses which, at first, runs parallel with the road on your left. When the track bends left in front of a post with a blue arrow, you should leave it to carry straight on, taking a wide path gently uphill and passing a golf green on your left. The path leads uphill through a copse to meet a track in front of a cottage. Turn right along the track and after a few paces when the track turns left into the car park for the windmill, bear right to follow a path which runs downhill. Almost immediately after joining, turn left onto a very narrow path which takes you around the front of the windmill where there are seats allowing you to enjoy the views across to the North Downs.

The windmill which ceased operating in the 19th century has now been converted into a church where services are held once a month.

⅓ mile

(2) Continue to bear left passing in front of the clubhouse and then turn right along the drive. After approximately twenty metres, turn right onto a signposted Public Footpath marked by a yellow arrow, going down some steps. You should then follow a prominent path downhill and go straight across a green, heading for a cottage the other side. Take a path to the left of the cottage marked by a blue "GW" arrow to continue between fields. On entering a field, follow a grass track across the centre and at the far side, fork left to continue along a track, now following a stream on your right. On reaching Dunsgate Farm, carry straight on along a lane which passes through the centre of the farmyard and after the last building on your left, turn left onto a signposted public footpath, following a fence on your right.

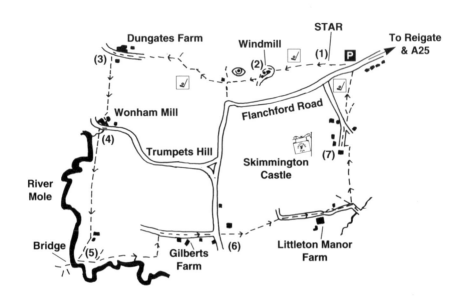

(3) Go over a stile into a field and continue in the same direction across the field and on entering another field, maintain your route heading for a large building in front of you which is Wonham Mill. On reaching the mill, turn left to cross the mill race and follow a grass path between the old mill house and the mill pond.

1 mile

(4) You will soon meet a lane where you should turn right and on reaching the mill buildings once more, take a signposted footpath opposite, crossing a bridge over a stream. Cross a field, passing to the left of a pillbox, and to the right of a second at the far side. Cross the next field keeping to the lefthand side and two thirds of the way across, pass to the right of a house. After this you should bear diagonally right across the centre of the field, to go over a stile beside a pillbox at the far side. — now 'no footpath'!

1¼ miles

<table>
<tr><td>1¾ miles</td><td>

(5) Turn left along a track, going away from the River Mole and bridge on your right. Pass behind a pillbox and after this, go over a stile on your right into a field. Go straight across the field with the river on your right and fencing on your left, and when the gap between the fencing and the river narrows, go over a stile on your left into another field. The stile is easily missed and as a guide, is in front of yet another pillbox. Turn right along the field edge and follow the perimeter round to eventually meet a track. Turn right along the track to soon pass Gilbert's Farm.

</td></tr>
<tr><td>2¼ miles</td><td>

(6) Cross a lane and follow a signposted public footpath the other side, which runs alongside Littleton's Nursing Home. The path leads to a field which you must cross in the direction of a footpath sign and at the far side, go over a stile beside a gate to follow a track ahead which leads to Littleton Manor Farm. The wooded hill in the distance, behind the farm, is Priory Park, the other side of which is the busy Reigate town centre. Pass to the left of Littleton Manor Farm and go over a stile ahead into a field. Do not follow the driveway in front of the farmhouse as this is private property. Continue ahead following the edge of the field and join the drive beside a barn. Turn left along the drive until it bends right, where you should leave it to take a signposted public bridleway to Reigate Heath on your left. This is the path which leads uphill between fields and not the path which runs diagonally left across a field on your left. Follow the bridleway over the hill and then to the right of The Skimmington Castle pub. Just after this, take a marked path left to arrive in front of the pub.

</td></tr>
</table>

<table>
<tr><td>2⅔ miles</td><td>

(7) From the pub, follow the tarmac lane which leads downhill away from the pub and when a track joins from the right, pass this to take the next track right (a few paces on), opposite a cottage on your left. This is also just before you reach a lamp post and postbox. Pass a golf green on your left and fork left just after, along a narrow path which enters the woodland of Reigate Heath. Keep to the path as it winds through the wood to lead back to the

</td></tr>
<tr><td>2¾ miles</td><td>

car park, our starting point,. which is reached by passing between some white posts.

</td></tr>
</table>

Nearby Attractions

Reigate Hill - Reigate. Famous hill on the North Downs affording good views.

Reigate. Ancient town with scant remains of a Norman castle and an attractive park, once the grounds of an old priory.

The Villagers
- Blackheath

Free House. A comfortable village pub consisting of one large carpeted bar. The low ceiling is dominated by wooden beams, many of which are used for chalking up special offers (both drink and food). A variety of prints and various knick-knacks from the past adorn painted white walls. At the rear is a large garden which backs onto the heath, popular with walkers. If you do not feel like conversation, the pub has Sky T.V. with regular showings of live sporting events. The pub offers an extensive range of home cooked food which includes some particularly good puddings. If you want to make a weekend of it, accommodation is available in the form of four chalet-style bedrooms.

 *11.00am-3.00pm, 6.00pm-11.00pm*

Beers: Brakspears - Bitter
           Courage - Best
           Wadsworth - 6X

Terrain

Mainly pine heathland. All the paths are well used, the biggest difficulty being navigating as there are so many of them. There are no steep gradients.

Getting to the Start (Grid Ref. 036462)

The walk starts from the car park at Blackheath village. Blackheath is best reached from the B2128 at Wonersh, or the A248 at Chilworth from where Blackheath is signposted. At a crossroads at the village centre, take the eastern road which is beside the Blackheath village sign. Follow the road past the Villagers pub and when it bends left, continue straight on to enter the car park.

The Walk

(1) Walk to the end of the car park and take the path which forks to the right of a Blackheath Common information sign. Go over a prominent crossing path and continue ahead with a heather clearing on your left and pine woodland on your right. As the path begins to descend you will meet a second crossing path. This too you should cross to after a few paces, meet a particularly wide path on to which you should turn left. Stay on this path (marked by blue topped posts and the number 303) until you eventually arrive at a lane beside a weatherboarded cottage on your right with a map of the heath on your left.

¾ mile
(2) As you meet the lane turn left on to a track and immediately after fork right, keeping to the track which is marked by blue posts and a yellow footpath arrow. The track soon forks again and you should keep right, the track now following the fence to a young plantation on your right. Look out for a marked footpath on your right and take this, thereby leaving the track to pass to the right of the beautiful Mustard Cottage. Continue until you meet a crossing path marked with a post and blue bridleway arrow and here turn left to go up uphill. The path soon levels out and at the same time widens to run in a straight line across the heath. Do not be tempted to turn off. The path goes over many crossing paths and tracks before eventually bending gently left in front of a post with two blue bridleway arrows. Do not to turn off but keep to the main path ignoring another crossing path a few paces on, also marked with a post and bridleway arrow. A short distance on the track bends left again with two paths joining from the right. Once again, keep to the main path (now a track) and continue to later go over another crossing track and ignore any further turnings off until you arrive at a large junction of paths and tracks.

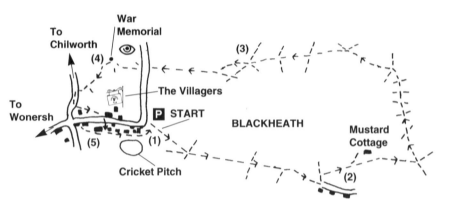

(3) Maintain your route by taking the second path from the right to shortly pass between some wooden rails and follow a prominent path along the edge of a heather clearing. Go over another crossing path (232) and continue ahead, shortly arriving at a large junction of tracks. Turn right at this point onto path P1 and follow it to later cross a lane, after which the path forks. Take the lefthand fork, thereby continuing straight on. The path leads to a large heather clearing with a stone cross, a War Memorial, on your right. Turn right to walk up to the War Memorial where you will have good views ahead of St. Martha's church.

1¼ miles

(4) At the War Memorial turn left and follow a narrow but prominent path across the heather clearing. On passing a white topped post, bear right, and keep to the path until you reach a lane. Turn left along the lane and after about 30 metres turn left again onto a narrow path marked with a blue topped post and number 301. The path passes behind a large house before taking you back onto the heath, to eventually arrive at The Villagers pub.

2 miles

(5) From the pub cross the road and join a path opposite, which runs between gardens and then on meeting a track turn left. Pass Blackheath cricket pitch and after the last house on the left keep to the track as it bends left, to arrive at the entrance of the car park, our starting point.

2½ miles

2½ miles

Nearby Attractions
St. Martha's church. Famous church at the to of St. Martha's Hill, once believed to be the site where Pagan Saxons executed early Christians.

The Abinger Hatch - Abinger Common

Free House. A beautiful 17th century inn facing the village church and pond with resident geese. The inn has a large split level bar, the lower level retaining its flagstone floor. Two real fires, one of which sits in the centre of the bar, keep you warm in Winter. The seating is a mixture of chairs and wooden benches, some of which are padded. The inn has a separate restaurant, though the bar meals are extensive and more than adequate for most. If you enjoy the pub during the day, you may wish to return for one of their popular live music evenings. The inn has a large garden.

 *11.00am-2.30pm, 6.00pm-11.00pm*

Beers: Badger - Best Bitter, Tanglefoot
              Ringwood - Best Bitter
              Wadsworth - 6X
              Guest Beers

Terrain

Mainly woodland paths and tracks with a small amount of lane walking. Some of the paths can be muddy, and in a couple of places the route is fairly steep. Abinger Common is a beautiful and unspoilt village.

Getting to the Start (Grid Ref. 126457)

The walk starts from the public car park at Friday Street. To get there, from the A25 west of Wotton or the B2126, follow the signs to Friday Street. The car park is well signposted. Please do not attempt to park at the pub as there is only room for a few cars and the public car park is only a few minutes walk away.

The Walk

(1) To start, walk to the entrance of the car park and then follow a path on your left that runs along the top of a bank beside the lane. When the path meets the lane, continue in the same direction along the lane, ignoring a signposted footpath on your right. Soon after take a marked path on the right that runs parallel with the lane. This is immediately after passing a second track marked 'Private Wotton Estate' on the same side. If you miss this path simply take the next turning right a little later on which is signposted as a Public Bridleway. The path now bends away from the lane and runs in a straight line through a wood to meet another lane.

(2) Turn right to follow the lane downhill (notice the old gate posts) and take the first lane on your left. The lane crosses a valley passing the Old Rectory on the way, before ending at a "T" junction at Abinger Common. The Abinger Hatch pub is on your right. *The pub, church, duck pond and green with stocks (supposedly never used), is a model village scene. One that has been carefully sculptured over the centuries as Abinger Common is reputedly the oldest village in England after the discovery of a Mesolithic pit dwelling. The model scene was almost destroyed in 1944 when the church was hit by a flying bomb. The church, incidentally, is dedicated to St. James, the patron saint for pilgrims, the Pilgrim's Way runs close by.*

½ mile

(3) From the pub cross the road and head for the church. At the entrance to the churchyard (do not enter) turn left, following the churchyard wall and at the far side of the green cross a lane and go up some steps to enter a field. Go straight across the field and at the other side go over a stile to enter Pasture Wood. Descend

¾ mile

along a narrow path for about 23 paces and then turn right onto an even narrower path, continuing your descent. You will notice in places some yellow paint marks on trees, indicating you are on a Public Footpath. On meeting a "T" junction (a wider path) beneath some electricity wires, turn right. The path continues in a straight line along the bottom of a valley and after a short distance widens to become a track. Do not be tempted to turn off but keep to the track which later bends left passing behind the houses of Holmbury St. Mary. It eventually leads to a gate and stile which you should cross to meet a junction of paths with a track on your right.

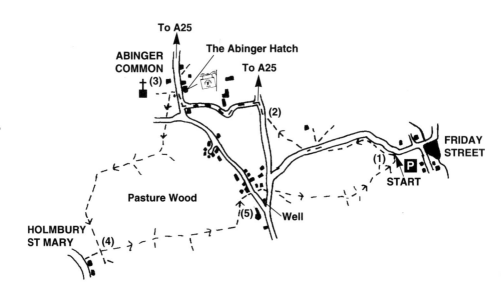

1½ miles **(4)** Go over a stile on your left and follow a narrow path steeply uphill. On nearing the top you should continue ahead along a wide strip of grass which cuts across the centre of Pasture Wood. Do not be tempted to turn off but follow the grass strip to its end, where you should maintain your route following a narrow path downhill. Go over a crossing track to follow a fenced path which runs between a field and a garden and leads to a lane at the southern end of Abinger Common.

At the southern end of a small green sits a well preserved village well. A large house facing the green, Goddards, was built as a rest house for 'ladies of small means', and was commissioned by the head of the Union Castle Shipping Line. The house was designed by the famous Surrey architect, Sir Edwin Lutyen.

(5) Cross the lane and follow a track which runs along the edge of the green and after passing the entrance to a couple of cottages, fork right along a narrow path to meet another lane. Cross the lane and follow a prominent path ahead, once more entering woodland and after about 20 metres fork left. After a couple of twists the path runs virtually in a straight line through the wood, becoming more prominent as you go. Keep to the main path and do not be tempted to turn off. Eventually, after descending a gentle slope you arrive at a junction of paths. Go straight across a crossing path that descends from a bank on your right, and at the other side fork right, following a prominent path gently uphill. After going under a line of electricity wires you will come to another junction of paths where you should turn first left. The path soon meets and follows the electricity wires you passed under earlier. Do not turn off but keep to the main path which then bears right, passing under the electricity wires to descend between banks. On meeting a lane turn left up some steps and follow a path back to the car park, our starting point. NB: turning right at the lane and then right again at a pond will bring you to the Stephan Langton, another featured pub.

2 miles

2¾ miles

Nearby Attractions
Leith Hill N.T. The highest hill in the south east of England, complete with viewing tower.

The Anchor
- Pyrford Lock

Courage. The pub's location is it's success. Once an overnight stop for canal traffic, the building has been enlarged and recently refurbished to become a popular waterside pub. The designers have made the most of the location. There is a large patio and a garden from where you can watch the colourful narrow-boats idling their way through the water. If it's raining there is a large conservatory from where you can watch the canal traffic in the dry, and the downstairs bar has large patio windows also overlooking the canal. If you get fed up watching the canal traffic there is a good range of games machines to keep you amused. The decor, as you would expect, is based around the artistry unique to the canal. There is a good range of pub food available which is managed through a loudspeaker system. Children are welcome, except in the main bar.

 *11.00am-3.00pm, 6.00pm-11.00pm*

Beers: Courage - Best Bitter, Directors
John Smith - Bitter

Terrain

Flat. Much of the walk is alongside the Wey Navigation Canal and the River Wey. Consequently, the going can get very muddy in wet weather.

Getting to the Start (Grid Ref. 066589)

The walk starts from Wisley Common Wrens Nest Car Park which is almost opposite the entrance to the Royal Horticultural Gardens. The easiest way to get there is via the A3 north of Guildford. The gardens are signposted from the northbound carriageway. Leaving the A3, do not go into the first car park on your left but follow the signs for Wisley village. The car park is the second on the right before you enter the village, signposted as Wisley Common Wrens Nest Car Park.

The Walk

(1) To start, walk out of the car park onto the lane, do not cross the lane but turn right and after a few paces take a narrow path on your right which leads into the wooded Wisley Common. Keep to the main path which in places is marked by yellow arrows on wooden posts, do not be tempted to turn off. Later, fork left still following the yellow arrows to eventually arrive at a crossing path with the M25 in front of you. Turn left and go over a stile, across a track to follow a prominent grass path ahead, again marked by yellow arrows and heading for Wisley village. After going over a stile, turn left along a concrete drive to arrive at a road at Wisley village.

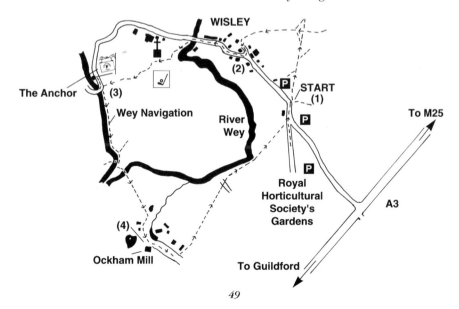

½ mile

(2) Cross the road and turn right to follow the pavement. After passing over the River Wey turn left onto a Public Footpath and after going over a stile onto a golf course turn right along a wide gravel path. On reaching a tarmac drive turn left and after a short distance turn right onto a track that winds its way across the golf course. When the track eventually ends a footpath continues alongside the car park to The Anchor pub before arriving at a lane and the pub itself.

The canal, known at this point as the Wey Navigation was opened in 1816 and linked the River Wey with the River Arun in Sussex, forming a route from the Thames to the south coast. The canal is now managed by the National Trust and the Wey and Arun Canal Trust who are step by step restoring the canal.

1¼ miles

(3) Turn left to follow the tow path alongside the canal. After passing a bridge over the canal, continue along the tow path for a further 50 metres and then turn left onto a path marked by a yellow arrow on a wooden post. This will shortly take you over the river Wey once more and then runs along the perimeter of the golf course. The path is well used and can be very muddy in wet weather. It eventually widens to become a track and after passing an ornamental lake on your left, bends right and continues, to arrive at Ockham Mill.

2¼ miles

(4) Follow the track round the front of the mill, going over the mill race, then go over a stile to follow a tarmac lane ahead. After a few paces turn left onto a signposted Public Footpath. This at first runs alongside a thick garden fir hedge before continuing in a straight line between fields. Cross a drive and take the footpath at the other side which follows the perimeter fencing to the Royal Horticultural Society Gardens. After meeting and following the river Wey for a stretch, the path becomes fenced on both sides and continues through the centre of the Society Gardens to eventually come out at a concrete drive beside a cottage. Turn left along the drive, then when you meet the pavement continue along it to arrive back at the Wrens Nest Car Park.

3 miles

Nearby Attractions
Royal Horticultural Society Gardens. Experimental gardens open to the public. The gardens are often a feature of horticultural programmes on television.

The Cyder House Inn - Shackleford

Shackleford Brewery Company/Free House. This unique pub is Surrey's only pub brewery hidden amongst the maze of lanes that enter the charming Shackleford village. The Cyder House Inn is a discovery that you will surely value. The simple plush carpeted 'C' shape bar is furnished with new but sturdy pine furniture which matches the pine bar. In the right side bar is a real fire and a glass door allowing patrons to observe the beer being brewed. The left bar area has a serving hatch for food which has a reputation equal to the pub's excellent beer. Beer connoisseurs will especially enjoy The Cyder House for, apart from it's own ale, the pub serves up to five other well kept beers and, as the name suggests, is only one of a handful of Surrey pubs offering real cider.

OPEN 11.30am - 3.00pm, 5.30pm - 11.00pm

Beers: Badgers - Best, Tanglefoot
                 Shackleford - Piston Broke, Old Shackle
                 Wadsworth - 6X

Beers: Guest Beers

Many bottled beers

Cider: Bulmers - Traditional

Symonds - Scrumpy Jack

Terrain

Woodland tracks and open fields. Gentle rolling countryside with no steep gradients.

Getting to the Start (Grid Ref. 921461)

The walk starts from the Puttenham Common car park, which is signposted as well as being marked on the Ordnance Survey Map. To get there make your way to Puttenham village and take the road opposite The Good Intent pub. After approximately 1¼ miles the lane bends sharp right in front of a cottage, where the entrance to the car park, which is signposted, is on your right. Alternatively, take the B3001, and just to the west of Elstead, take a road signposted to Puttenham. Go straight on at a crossroads, passing Cutt Mill Ponds and continue until the lane bends sharp left in front of a cottage where you will see the car park on your left.

The Walk

(1) From the car park follow the track which you entered by, out of the car park and then cross the road passing to the right of a cottage to join a signposted footpath which runs alongside the cottage. On meeting a sunken path, turn right to shortly pass some pretty cottages on your left. After the cottages continue ahead along a lane to pass Rodsall Manor and then take a signposted bridleway left.

¼ mile **(2)** You should now keep to a sandy track, ignoring all turnings off until you eventually reach a "T" junction in the midst of a pretty wood marked by a post and some blue bridleway arrows. Turn left at the "T" junction onto a wide path and follow it gently uphill until you reach a junction of tracks marked by another post, this time with several red arrows. Maintain your route ahead now following a track gently uphill (do not make the mistake of taking the track left). When the track bends right leave it to go over a stile into a field. The view ahead now is of Shackleford village. Go diagonally right across the field heading for a stile, approximately 2/3 of the way down the field perimeter on your right. Go over the stile and turn left along a lane to meet another stile on your left approximately 50 metres on. To visit the pub continue along the lane to a "T" junction at the village centre. Turn right and follow the road to the Village Stores, where you should take the road opposite to reach The Cyder House Inn. You will have to retrace your steps to the stile to continue the route.

(3) The footpath passes to the left of a house and proceeds along the edge of two fields before joining a track beside a cottage. Continue ahead passing some more cottages to arrive at a "T" junction and then turn right, downhill, past Lydling Farm to arrive at a road beside a pond.

1½ miles

(4) Turn left along the road until you see a stile on your left beside a gate. Go over this stile followed by a quick succession of stiles to enter a field and continue straight ahead, going uphill along the edge of the field. At the far corner maintain your route straight on, now following a narrow path which runs alongside a fence on your left. The fence ends on reaching a junction of paths where you should continue straight ahead to shortly go down a bank onto a sunken path. Turn left and after fifteen paces turn right and retrace your steps to the car park, our starting point.

2 miles

3 miles

Nearby Attractions

Cuttmill Ponds. A line of ponds set in open heathland, popular with families in Summer.

Seale Village. An attractive village below the Hogs Back with a popular craft complex.

Waverley Abbey. Managed by English Heritage, the Abbey is now reduced to a romantic ruin.

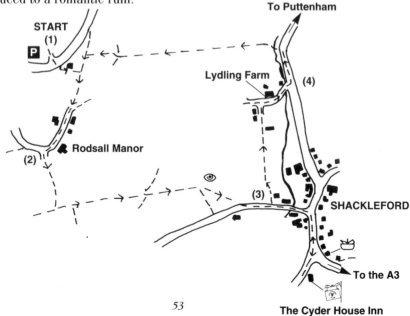

53

The Crown Inn
- Chiddingfold

Hotel. The Crown Inn or "Le Crounne" as it was originally known was built in 1258 as a rest place for travelling pilgrims and Cistercian Monks. It is without competition the oldest inn in Surrey and possibly England. The fine half timbered Wealden building is much photographed and once over the threshold, the picture is even better. Panelled walls and huge oak beams preserve the memory of Edward VI and Elizabeth I, past guests at the inn. On the way to the bar you pass a public telephone cleverly sited in a Sedan chair. The bar is comfort itself, a thick carpet covers the floor with lounge chairs informally arranged around wooden tables, some of which are centuries old. At one end, framed by huge oak beams, is a large stone fireplace well used in Winter. The windows, as you would expect from an ancient glassmaking centre, include panes of stained glass. Bar food is available, but if you can afford it, the separate restaurant is more than worth a try. Its reputation is justifiably excellent. Better still, why not stay over in one of the original bedrooms where the four-poster beds are so heavy it would be almost impossible to ever move them.

⊠, ¡O¡, ⊼, 🛏, OPEN *11.00am-3.00pm, 5.30pm-11.00pm*

Beers: Badger - Best Bitter, Tanglefoot
Hall & Woodhouse (brewers of Badger Beers) - Hard Tackle
Wadsworth - 6X
Guest Beer

Terrain

A gentle walk through fields and deciduous woodland with a small amount of road walking. In wet weather, some of the paths can be particularly muddy so wear good shoes.

Getting to the Start (Grid Ref.961355)

The walk starts from in front of The Crown which faces the village green. Chiddingfold is on the A283 south of Godalming. There is a small parking area in front of the shops beside the Crown. Alternatively, street parking is possible on the roads which skirt the green.

Chiddingfold was once a famous glass making centre, providing the stained glass for windows in Westminster Abbey and St. Georges Chapel, Windsor. The green is home to a popular Summer fair and one of the largest Guy Fawkes bonfires in the county.

The Walk

(1) Facing The Crown, take the alleyway to the left that runs between the inn and the newsagents. Turn left along the main road passing The Swan pub, then follow the main road over a stream, cross the small cul-de-sac, Turners Mead, and after the last house on the left, turn left onto a signposted Public Footpath.

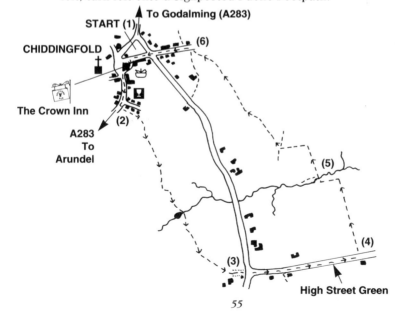

(2) The path at first runs behind some houses, then after going over a stile continues ahead along the righthand edge of a field. At the far side of the field go over a stile and follow a well used path uphill through a wood. Go over another stile and then turn left to follow the field edge. At the field corner go over a stile and follow a fenced path through a wood. The path descends by some steps to reach a pond which used to power the glass works for which Chiddingfold was famous. After the pond keep to the path to go over a stile into a field and continue ahead along the field edge. At the far side pass through a gate, turn immediately left and pass through a second gate into another field, then follow the righthand edge of this field which means, for much of the way, walking along the top of a grass bank. On reaching the corner of the field go over a stile on your right and then turn left down a tarmac drive to reach a road.

(3) Cross the road and follow the road the other side, "High Street Green". The road is straight and reasonably quiet and has a good grass verge on which you can safely walk. Follow the road for approximately half a mile until you see a signposted Public Footpath on your left, this is just after passing a small wooden cottage on your right.

(4) The path cuts a straight line through woodland following a line of electricity poles. After going down some steps the path descends to join another path onto which you should turn left. Go over a stream via a wooden footbridge and turn left to enter a field.

(5) Turn right to follow the field edge and on reaching the corner continue along the edge of the field until you reach a gap in the hedge on your right, marked by a wooden post with yellow footpath arrows. Pass through the gap into another field, then proceed ahead going diagonally left across the field, to reach a stile at the lefthand perimeter. The stile is slightly hidden and, as a guide, is a few metres to the right of quite a wide gap in the hedge. Go over a stile into another field and go straight across the field, at the far side passing through a strip of woodland to enter yet another field. Maintain your route by going across the centre of the field, and at the far side go over a stile into a smaller field (our last field). Cross this heading for the far righthand corner.

(6) Go over a stile and turn left along a lane, past the first houses of Chiddingfold and the village Post Office before arriving at a crossroads. Continue straight on following the road ahead along the edge of the village green to arrive back at The Crown Inn, our starting point.

The Kings Head
- Holmbury St. Mary

Free House. Overlooked by a small green, The Kings Head is an out of the way pub and all the better for it. The bar has two distinct halves. The front half is carpeted and has a large rack holding newspapers for the patron who simply wants a quiet drink. The rear is bare floorboards and exposed walls with sturdy pine furniture, including a large table and benches, convenient for a large group. There is pool and bar billiards for games enthusiasts. Throughout the pub there are exposed beams with hops hanging from the ceiling. On the walls there are some interesting pictures, including many scenes of African life. Two real fires make the pub an ideal place to spend a Winter's day and in Summer you can enjoy a cool drink in a pleasant sloping garden. Food-wise, the pub has a good selection of bar meals.

✕, ⅂, *11.00am-3.00pm, 6.00pm-11.00pm (All day Sat.)*

Beers: Brakspears - Best Bitter
Fullers - London Pride
Ringwood - Best Bitter, Old Thumper

Terrain

The majority of the route is along woodland paths and tracks. The walk can be strenuous in places, with a steep descent at one point to reach Holmbury St. Mary and a steady climb after visiting the pub. The scenery is stunning throughout, with the finale (apart from the pub) being the views from Holmbury Hill Fort.

Getting to the Start (Grid Ref. 099431)

The walks starts from Hurtwood Control car park number 1 on the side of Holmbury Hill. Unless you have local knowledge, the best way to get there is to make your way to Peaslake and from there take Radnor Road, the road opposite the butchers. The car park, which is well signposted, is approximately one and a quarter miles along the road on the lefthand side. Occasionally the gates to the car park are locked. If this is the case when you visit, there is plenty of alternative car parking along the road.

The Walk

(1) To start, from the car park with your back to the road, leave the car park by taking a track opposite the car park entrance, passing to the right of a stone charity donation box. After a few paces, leave the track by forking left onto a narrow path. On meeting another track, turn right for a few paces before turning left onto another track. This is an extremely wide track and after a short distance, another track joins it from the right. You should keep to the track to go gently downhill and disregard any turnings off. You will eventually meet a junction where two wide tracks join from the left with another track on the right. Carry straight on here, keeping to the track you are already on, to take the next track right which is approximately 75 metres further on.

¾ mile   (2) Follow the track uphill and go over a crossing track to continue in a straight line through the Hurtwood. On reaching a second wide crossing track, continue straight on to join a narrow path the other side which leads downhill, twisting as it goes. Near the bottom, go over a wide crossing path, continuing your descent, to soon come out on to a drive way to a house on your right. Follow the drive ahead to reach a lane in front of some pretty cottages.

The cottages are part of Holmbury St. Mary which, despite its ancient appearance, is essentially a Victorian village. The village church which you meet further on was built in 1873 and was designed by G.E.Street who lived at Holmbury, whose most famous work is the London Law Courts.

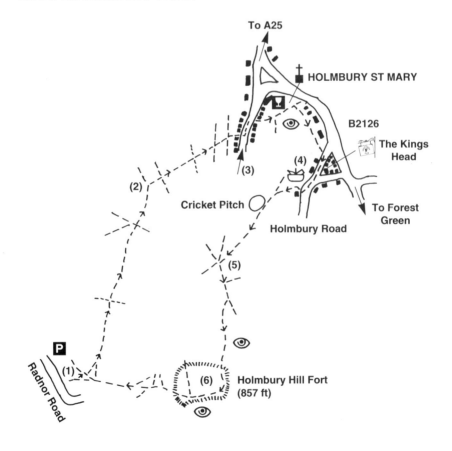

(3) Turn left along the lane and after about 30 metres, leave it and take a track on your right. The track bends slowly round to the left to arrive at a small parking area and tarmac lane. Turn right here, going up some steps, and fork left following a holly hedge to soon enter a churchyard. Once in the churchyard, fork right taking the higher path which runs along the top of the churchyard and exit the other side via a wooden gate. After this, follow a narrow path behind some houses and fork left when you meet a pair of electricity poles supporting a mini generator, to shortly meet a lane. Turn right along the lane which will soon lead you to The Kings Head pub.

1 mile

1¼ miles **(4)** From the pub, take the higher lane which runs alongside the green and at the end of the green, turn right onto Holmbury Road. A few paces after, turn right onto a track, signposted to Holmbury St. Mary Cricket Club and follow this uphill past the cricket pitch to its end at a large junction of tracks.

1¾ miles **(5)** Take the first turning on your left, a track marked by a blue "GW" arrow. Sometime later, fork right passing to the right of a wooden footpath post and follow a prominent path and where applicable, the "GW" arrows, to eventually reach the top of Holmbury Hill. *This is identifiable by a stone memorial seat and direction finder. Holmbury Hill Fort dates from the Iron Age and is one of several along the Greensand Ridge. When in use, the surrounding banks would have been strengthened by a wooden or stone wall. Holmbury Hill Fort is fairly small and was probably only a temporary stronghold, used mainly to harbour animals.*

2½ miles **(6)** Go straight across the top of the hill to join a path the other side marked by a blue "GW" arrow and follow the main path ahead ignoring any turnings off. Fork left after passing a green memorial seat and at the next fork take the righthand path and shortly after, turn left along a sandy track. Keep to the track and when a large junction of tracks comes into view ahead, separated from the track you are on by some wide concrete posts, take the left hand fork. This, after a few paces, passes to the right of a pond after which, you should follow the track ahead to reach Hurtwood car 3 miles park number 1, our starting point.

Nearby Attractions

Leith Hill N.T. The highest hill in the South East of England, complete with viewing tower.

The Sportsman
- Mogador

Courage. This delightful 16th century pub was once a Royal hunting lodge. Today, set on the edge of Walton Heath, The Sportsman is a welcome haven from the burgeoning suburbs of London. Thankfully the pub has stood still whilst the 20th century accelerates at an alarming pace around it. Walk through the door and apart from the electric lights you could be in the last century. There are two very snug bars, one carpeted and the other with stripped floorboards, there is a small real fire to keep you warm in Winter. The pub serves a good and imaginative range of home cooked food, which includes a number of daily specials. Outside, the pub overlooks a small dew pond where commoners once watered their animals. There is a rail where horse riders can tie their mounts. At the side and to the rear of the pub is a large garden with a collection of garden toys to entertain the kids.

 11.00am-3.00pm, 5.30pm-11.00pm

Beers: Courage - Best Bitter, Directors
            Wadsworth - 6X
            Guest Beer

Terrain

Nearly all the walk is on Walton Heath, a mixture of wood and open grassland. There are no steep ascents, but the lack of easily identifiable landmarks means you must pay careful attention to the route description.

Getting to the Start (Grid Ref. 246527)

The walk starts from the National Trust car park at Margery Wood. The car park is at the end of Margery Lane which is the first turning left on the south bound carriageway of the A217 after the junction with the M25.

The Walk

(1) Walk back to the entrance of the car park, then turn left and left again, onto a narrow path signposted as a bridleway, do not go over the stile or join the track. The bridleway eventually leads to a lane which you should cross and continue ahead to soon meet a second lane.

½ mile

(2) Turn left to immediately pass a cottage, Thornymoor, and continue until you reach a bridge over the motorway where you should turn right on to another signposted bridleway. This at first runs parallel with the motorway and then bends right to pass through a wood. Stick to the main path through the wood and ignore all the turnings off. You will soon see Walton Heath Golf Course on your left. The golf course is famous for staging the Ryder Cup in 1981. *As you continue notice a stout white post with a red cross on it. This is one of a series of posts which formed a 'coal' boundary around London. Any coal crossing this boundary was liable to extra duty.* Later you will meet a prominent crossing path with another white toll post ahead of you. Maintain your route by crossing the path and continue to ignore any further turnings off. Keeping to the main path you will eventually come out at the open grassland of Walton Heath.

1¼ miles

(3) Bear left here on a hedged path which runs between the Golf Course on your left and the grass heath on your right. As you continue you will notice you are still following the white toll posts.

1¾ miles

(4) When the path comes out to an open grass area with some woodland ahead, turn right to follow a wide grass track which

runs between the wood now on your left and a hedge on your right. This is often used by horses so take care, especially if you have dogs. The hedge on your right gives way in places to afford lovely views across the heath on your right. Look out for the square tower in the distance; this is the water tower at the top of Colley

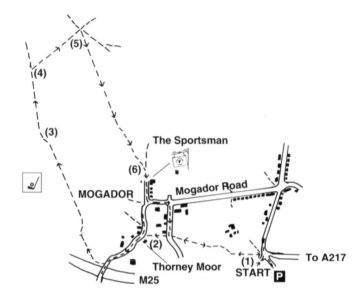

Hill.

2 miles

(5) You will eventually come to a wide junction of tracks. Here you should turn right on to a well-used grass track which leads gently downhill. To help you, there should now be a narrow strip of woodland and bracken on your left. At the bottom of a shallow valley the track passes through another strip of woodland. After this you should continue to follow the track across the heath; as before ignore all minor paths which crisscross the route. Eventually you will see 2 white posts and a white bar directly in front of you and you should head for this to arrive at The Sportsman.

2½ miles

(6) After The Sportsman, continue straight on along a lane and when this meets a road turn left. After about 30 metres you should take another lane right; this is called Margery Grove. Follow Margery Grove until you meet Laurel Cottage on your right and here turn left on to a signposted bridleway, the bridleway followed at the

3 miles

William IV
- Little London

Free House. You will rarely find such a distinctly rural pub so close to London. The main bar has a flagstone floor with a huge fireplace which is a blessing in Winter. Another small bar leads off to the rear. The furniture is solid tables and benches, some of which have been carved out of fallen trees. The painted brick walls are sparsely decorated with some old wood-cutters' swords and a number of old photographs, proving how little the pub has changed. On a slightly higher level is the restaurant with more seating upstairs when it gets busy. The food comes highly recommended, particularly good are the wide range of steaks which include a steak sandwich, convenient for the walker. Occasionally the landlord does a venison spit roast which is worth travelling a long way for. There is a small but pleasant garden at the front of the pub. The beers are changed regularly, those listed below are a typical selection.

✗, 🍽, ⅁, **OPEN**   *11.00am-3.00pm, 5.30pm-11.00pm*

Beers: Castle - Eden Ale
             Courage - Best
             Boddingtons - Bitter
             Flowers - Original

Terrain

Paths and tracks, mainly through open parkland with some wooded sections. Gentle rolling countryside with no steep gradients.

Getting to the Start (Grid Ref. 060485)

The walk starts from the Silent Pool car park, situated on the northern side of the A25 between Guildford and Shere, almost opposite the turn off for the A248. The car park is well signposted.

The Walk

Before you start you may want to visit the Silent Pool with its ghost and connections with King John. There is also an animal farm here called Sherbourne Farm, ideal for children.

(1) From the car park cross the A25 with care, turning left the other side and then right to follow the A248 signposted to Godalming and Albury. There is a pavement on the lefthand side of the road which you can take. Ignore a marked footpath and continue to follow the road passing along the way the Apostolic Church and after crossing the Tillingbourne river, turn left onto New Road, signposted to Albury Heath, Farley Green and Peaslake. The Apostolic Church was built in the mid-19th century on the instructions of Henry Drummond, the then owner of Albury Park. It was built to serve a new Christian sect which believed that the second advent of Christ was near. The church is private and no longer used.

(2) Pass a pretty stone house on your left and immediately after turn   ½ mile
left onto the drive to Albury Park. The park is private so please do not wander off the drive. There are some lovely views over the Tillingbourne river on your left as you progress. When the drive forks, take the lefthand drive and when it begins to bend left continue straight on across a small green to visit the old redundant church of St. Peter & St. Paul. *To the right of the church you can see the old manor house. The church is originally Saxon and fell into disuse when the Lord of Manor, preferring his own company, evicted the villagers from their homes moving them to the current Albury village. Today the church is maintained by the Redundant Churches Fund and inside there are some interesting remains including a brass to John de Weston, circa*

1440. The church is in a lovely position overlooking the Tillingbourne, the Park which includes some magnificent Redwood trees, is said to have been designed by the famous diarist John Evelyn of Wotton. There are some good booklets available inside the church, detailing its history.

¾ mile **(3)** Leave the church via the same entrance by which you arrived, then walk back across the green and on reaching a gravel drive just before the tarmac one, turn left to cross an area of grass, go over another tarmac drive and proceed uphill heading for a small gate and footpath sign. Pass through the gate and follow a prominent path ahead still going uphill. On meeting a track turn left and follow this over the top of the hill through an area of newly planted woodland which replace the trees damaged in the storm of 1987. Maintain your route, ignoring all turnings off including a number of crossing tracks (if in doubt follow the yellow arrows). Eventually, after passing through an area of mature woodland which would fit well into any Grimms fairytale, the track twists left to meet another track where you should turn right. You will shortly pass to the left of a house (South Lodge) where you should leave the Park by passing through a metal gate onto a road. Cross the road and follow a track ahead which passes a number of magnificent houses (ignoring tracks off to the left) before arriving at another road and the William IV pub.

1½ miles **(4)** After the pub, retrace your steps along the track to where you left Albury Park at South Lodge. This time do not re-enter the Park through the metal gates, but instead pass through a kissing gate to the right of the metal gates. Bear diagonally right following a fence on your right walking through an avenue of sweet chestnut trees. Your way is now downhill through an area of beautiful parkland with good views ahead of the North Downs. Keep following the fence on your right to eventually pass over a stile, maintaining your route ahead to shortly pass through a low kissing gate, coming out onto a sandy path beside a lovely tile hung cottage on your right. You may have noticed, like this cottage, many of the buildings en route are painted in the same colour green. This is because they all belong to the Albury Estate.

2¼ miles **(5)** Turn left to cross over the Tillingbourne (if you want to visit Shere then turn right just before the Tillingbourne and follow the path beside the river into the village). After crossing the Tillingbourne follow the narrow tarmac lane ahead passing to the right of a 'chocolate box' half timbered house and continue until you see a signposted crossing path. Turn left here going up a bank to shortly enter a field. Maintain your route across the centre of the field heading for the far corner, on your left you will see the old walls of the Albury Estate. At the corner pass through a gate to follow a prominent path ahead through a small area of woodland. After a short descent leave the wood via a stile, following a prominent path ahead across a field. If the way is unclear, head just to the right of the church in front of you, to your left you will be able to make out the earlier part of our route through Albury Park and in Winter when the trees are bare you can just see the old church. At the far side of the field go over another stile and follow a track ahead to meet the A248. Turn right and retrace your route to the Silent Pool car park, our starting point.

3 miles

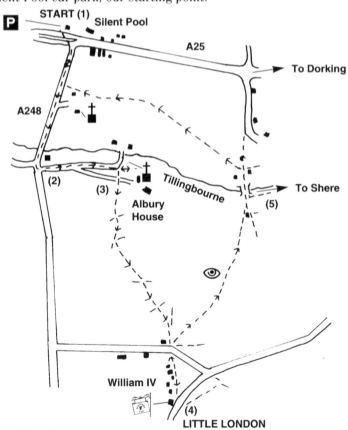

Nearby Attractions

St. Martha's Church. Famous church at the top of St. Martha's Hill, once believed to be the site where Pagan Saxons executed early Christians.

Distance 3¼ miles   **Level B**

Ordnance Survey Landranger Map 187

𝔗𝔥𝔢 ℭ𝔯𝔦𝔠𝔨𝔢𝔱𝔢𝔯𝔰
- 𝔚𝔢𝔰𝔱𝔠𝔬𝔱𝔱

Free House. A small local pub in a beautiful Surrey village, nestling below the North Downs. The one carpeted bar is split into three levels. The bottom level has a pool table and generally acts as a games area, with the top level, beside a serving hatch, naturally being used as an eating area. The central and larger level is mainly (but not just) for those who want to enjoy the pub's well kept beers. The pub offers some good bar meals which come in generous portions.

 11.00am-3.00pm, 5.30pm-11.00pm

Beers: Badger - Best Bitter, Tanglefoot
 Boddingtons - Bitter
 Brakspears - Bitter
 Fullers - London Pride

Terrain

Mainly along well used paths and tracks through woods and between fields. The scenery is particularly pretty and holds your interest, making the walk seem shorter than it is. Parts of the route are quite steep, so do not get too over confident.

68

Getting to the Start (Grid Ref. 141485)

The walk starts from in front of The Cricketers. Westcott is on the A25 between Dorking and Gomshall. Limited street parking is possible in the village and also along the lane leading from The Cricketers to the church, though please leave the area in front of the church entrance clear.

The Walk

(1) From The Cricketers' pub walk away from the A25 to take a signposted Public Footpath, also marked as Heath Rise. This takes the form of a narrow lane, passing some pretty cottages and houses on your left with heathland on your right. At the end of the lane turn left on to another signposted footpath, after approximately 20 metres turn right, passing through an old kissing gate on to another marked footpath. This runs between hedges and gardens and soon begins to climb uphill. Cross a lane and follow another narrow footpath the other side, now leaving the houses of Westcott behind to run between fields.

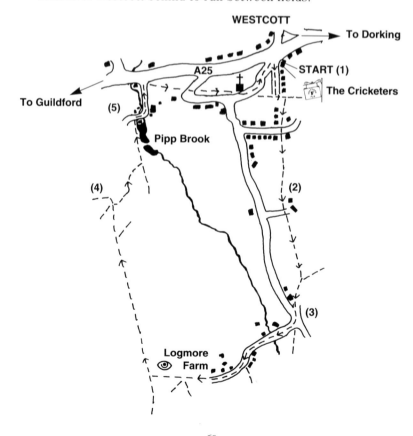

(2) Sometime on, this path meets a track which you should follow to continue ahead, passing some stables on your left. Shortly after, cross over a drive and continue ahead once more along a footpath between fields. Follow the path which climbs gently uphill, later affording open views left across to Ranmore and its church, as well as parts of Westcott. Soon after ignore a path off to your left beside two farm gates and continue ahead now along a track to shortly reach a lane.

(3) Cross the lane to join a track almost opposite with signposts to Logmore Green and Logmore Farm. It is also marked as a public bridleway. Stay on the track, passing a mixture of properties until it ends beside Logmore Farm. Here you should continue ahead, passing through a small wooden gate, to follow a path uphill. Pass two paths off to the left, keeping to the path you are on to reach the top of the hill where there are superb views back across Westcott and the surrounding countryside. Pass through a small wooden gate and turn right along a gravel track. The track later widens becoming sandy and continues downhill between banks. The trees on your left soon end and you will follow an open field on the same side for a short distance.

(4) When the fields on your left end and the track bends sharp left in front of a field gate, you should turn right instead to pass between wooden posts and join a narrow path marked by a yellow footpath arrow and as the Greensand Way (G.W.). The footpath winds through woodland descending to eventually pass through some more posts onto a wider path where you should turn left. The path runs alongside a field on your left and thereafter a line of modern houses on the same side.

(5) Turn right onto Rookery Drive to shortly pass through a picture book hamlet, complete with a fairytale waterfall. The waterfall is fed by Pipp Brook which once powered no less than six watermills. Follow the drive to its end beside Rookery Lodge, where you should turn right just before the main road on to a public footpath which is signposted. This is a narrow sandy path which runs uphill. At the top of the hill continue ahead to cross a lane and join a narrow footpath the other side which crosses the edge of Westcott Heath. When the path meets the lane again, in front of a graveyard, turn left following the lane downhill to The Cricketers pub, passing the village church on the way. *The church was built by Sir Gilbert Scott who also designed St. Pancras Station and The Albert Memorial.*

Nearby Attractions

Polesden Lacey N.T. A remodelled Regency villa, once home to the Hon.Mrs. Ronald Greville. King George VI and Queen Elizabeth the Queen Mother, spent some of their honeymoon here.

The Hurtwood Inn
- Peaslake

Free House. A large hotel which dominates one of the most secluded villages in Surrey. The hotel, once part of the THF chain, is now a private concern. The enthusiastic owners have made many improvements, designed to enhance your visit whether it be for an hour or a weekend. The carpeted horseshoe bar is comfort itself, the well padded lounge chairs entice you to stay for 'just one more'. The imaginative bar food comes highly recommended. There is a separate oak-panelled 'a la carte' and 'table D'hote' restaurant of which the owners are justifiably proud. In Summer you can enjoy these treats in a pleasant garden. All the bedrooms are being upgraded and by the time this book goes to print, all should have en suite facilities.

 *11.00am-3.00pm, 6.00pm-11.00pm*

Beers: Courage - Best Bitter
Gibbs Mew - Deacon, Wake
Wadsworth - 6X

Terrain

Nearly all the walk is through the famous Hurtwood which covers some 4,000 acres. There are no sharp ascents, but the first half of the walk to the highest point at Pitch Hill is a long steady climb. The reward (on a clear day) is some magnificent views. Like most woodland walks the going can be muddy.

Getting to the Start (Grid Ref. 087446)

The walk starts from The Hurtwood Inn at Peaslake, behind which is a public car park. Peaslake is well signposted from the A25 at Gomshall, the B2126 at Holmbury St. Mary and the B2127 at Ewhurst.

Peaslake, because of its 'tucked away' position remained one of the last smuggling strongholds in Surrey. In contrast, the village also has strong associations with the Quakers. The Quaker cemetery is passed at the beginning of the walk.

The Walk

(1) To start, facing The Hurtwood Inn, turn left along the lane and after a few paces, take a signposted public bridleway left, a tarmac drive which leads up to the village church. Follow the drive round behind the church and here leave the drive to take a signposted Public Footpath ahead. When the path meets the cemetery, continue straight ahead now along a track, passing to the left of the cemetery, to enter Hurtwood. A little later, ignore two tracks leading off to the right and continue until the track forks.

½ mile **(2)** Take the left fork and follow the track for approximately three quarters of a mile, ignoring all turnings off, to eventually pass to the left of a house. At this point, the track changes and becomes the drive way to the house and you should follow the drive until the perimeter hedge ends, where you should turn right onto a path marked by a blue "GW" arrow.

1¼ mile **(3)** Follow the path uphill to meet another track where you should turn left to pass behind a view seat. After this, fork left and follow a path along the edge of the hill. On reaching a junction of paths turn right to arrive at the top of Pitch Hill, identified by a trig point at the summit. The views from the hill are magnificent and on a clear day you can even see the South Downs. Pass to the right of the trig point and follow a wide path, leading away from the edge

72

of the hill. Keep to the main path (do not turn off) to later pass to the left of a quarry and go downhill to reach Hurtwood car park number 3.

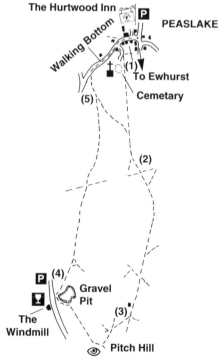

(4) Cross a track and go straight across the car park to join a path the other side which leads gently downhill. The path crosses a grass area and continues downhill through the Hurtwood. As before, keep to the main path ignoring all turnings off and later, when the path forks, fork left to continue downhill. After this, do not be tempted to take any further turnings off, but keep to the path to eventually join a track, where you should maintain your route ahead.

1¾ miles

(5) Follow the track, later passing a pond, to eventually enter a parking area. Go straight across the car park to reach a lane. Turn right along the lane and follow it back to Peaslake village centre and The Hurtwood Inn, our starting point.

2¾ miles

3¼ miles

Nearby Attractions
Gomshall. An attractive Surrey village famous for its leather.
Shere. A picture-book village with many craft shops and a small museum.

Distance 3¼ miles   **Level C**

Ordnance Survey Landranger Map 186

𝕿𝖍𝖊 𝕻𝖊𝖗𝖈𝖞 𝕬𝖗𝖒𝖘
- 𝕮𝖍𝖎𝖑𝖜𝖔𝖗𝖙𝖍

Greene King. A large friendly pub on the banks of the Tillingbourne River which runs through the pub garden. The Suffolk Brewery, Greene King, recently acquired the pub and completely refurbished it. The result is a spacious split level lounge with plenty of cosy corners, complemented by a large conservatory with views of the famous St. Martha's Hill. There is a games area and for a small fee, in Summer, you can enjoy a game of boule, the French equivalent of bowls, played on a gravel court. Good traditional pub food is served with daily specials. The pub also has a ghost which is affectionately called George.

, ✗, 💱, ♿, *OPEN 11.00am-3.00pm, 6.00pm-11.00pm*

Beers: Greene King - IPA, Rayments Special, Abbot Ale

Terrain

Mainly sandy, well trodden paths, through typical beautiful Surrey woodland with the added attraction of the Tillingbourne River. The paths along the banks of the river can get very muddy and the descent and climb of St. Martha's Hill is quite steep. This walk therefore, is not advisable if you are unfit.

Getting to the Start (Grid Ref. 035484)

The walk starts from the car park for St. Martha's Hill which is signposted as such. The car park is reached from Guildford Lane which runs from Albury to Guildford. From Guildford the Lane starts as Sidney Road and leads off Epsom Road, which is the A25 route into Guildford. You should follow the lane for approximately 2½ miles until you see the car park on your right. The other end of Guildford Lane leaves the A248 just west of Albury. The lane can also be identified by two 7.5 ton weight restriction signs. The car park, which is well marked, is shortly reached on the left. If you do not have a car, Chilworth Railway Station is opposite The Percy Arms

The Walk

(1) From the car park take a prominent path marked by a blue arrow to the left of a St. Martha's Hill information sign. The path soon bends right and meets a junction of paths and tracks. Carry straight on here on a wide sandy track going uphill. The track takes you all the way to the summit of the hill and St. Martha's church. To assist you in finding your route, there are a number of posts with a picture of a church beside the track. If you keep to the main track at all times and do not turn off you will get to the summit without difficulty. Along the way you will pass an old pill box and the start of the Downs Link path which runs from here to the South Downs, West Sussex.

St. Martha's Hill is 573 feet high and on a clear day it is meant to be possible to see parts of no less than eight counties. The church is originally Saxon which has been much altered over the centuries. In 1763 the tower collapsed as a result of an accident which involved a gunpowder explosion. The tower you see today was built in 1850. It is believed the name St. Martha's is derived from martyr and tradition has it that the hill was the site for execution of early Christians by Pagan Saxons.

(2) On meeting the churchyard wall take the path left which follows ½ mile
the wall round to the front of the church. At the front of the

church beside the churchyard entrance (which is between two yew trees), turn left to take a sandy path downhill which almost immediately follows a fence on your right to a small underground reservoir. Go over a crossing path and continue downhill. The path can be quite steep in places so take care. As you descend you will have good views on your right over Chilworth Manor. The path eventually comes out at a track where you should turn right. Turn left onto the gravel drive for Chilworth Manor to come out at a lane beside a gatehouse. Continue straight on along the lane, taking care when the lane bends sharp left as you will be hidden to traffic. The lane passes over a bridge where, to your right is a disused mill race from one of the old gunpower mills for which this part of Surrey was once famous.

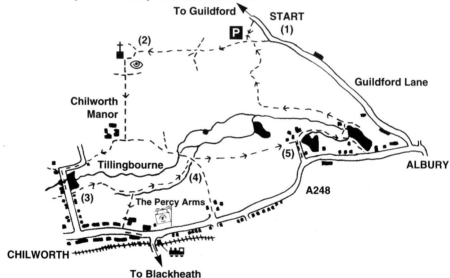

1¼ miles **(3)** Shortly after the bridge turn left passing through an iron gate to follow a path along the Tillingbourne River. As you join the path there is an information sign describing the gunpowder mills which once thrived along this part of the river. Along the way you will see scattered remains of this industry, including a large number of old millstones. Keep to the main path all the time, at one point going over a bridge, until the path forks, the righthand fork going over another bridge. To visit The Percy Arms, turn right at the righthand fork, going over the bridge and follow the path until you reach the main road the A248. Turn left and you will reach The Percy Arms. You will need to retrace your steps over the bridge to continue the route.

(4) Continue to follow the path to soon pass to the right of some of the largest remains of the old mills before arriving at a tarmac drive. Turn right to go over a bridge and then go over a stile on your left into a field. Cross the field in the direction of the footpath sign and on entering another field maintain your route following a ditch on your right which becomes a stream in wet weather. At the far side go over another stile, following the path ahead which passes to the right of a lake and after going over a stile, passes to the right of a house before coming out at a tarmac drive in front of a millpond. 2 mile

(5) Follow the drive left, keeping to the edge of the pond, passing to the right of the mill. The drive later bends left beside a second pond and ends at an entrance to a house on your left. Fork left here and take a narrow path which at first runs alongside the house and then above the Tillingbourne River. The path eventually bends right to begin the ascent of St. Martha's Hill which will be quite hard work if you have spent too long at The Percy Arms. Near the top, fork left keeping to the main path to come out at a sandy track. Turn left and at a junction of paths and tracks turn first right and follow a path back to the car park, our starting point. 2¾ mile

3¼ mile

Nearby Attractions
Guildford. Historic town with the remains of a Norman castle.
Clandon Park N.T. Large house built in the 1730's for the 2nd Lord Onslow.

𝕿𝖍𝖊 𝕲𝖔𝖔𝖉 𝕴𝖓𝖙𝖊𝖓𝖙
- 𝕻𝖚𝖙𝖙𝖊𝖓𝖍𝖆𝖒

Courage. A fine 16th century pub situated on the North Downs Way and therefore popular with walkers. A large 'C' shaped bar which is divided into three very different drinking areas. One section is reserved for pub games and has a pool table; there is a basic but comfortable public bar and a snug lounge with a magnificent inglenook fire which is a welcome comfort in cold weather. The lounge has many exposed beams and cosy corners with a segregated area often used by people ordering food. Overall, it is a very relaxing and friendly pub and one to which you will want to return. Apart from the regular beers, the pub normally has three Guest ales, the landlord enthusiastically displays future beers on the blackboard at the bar.

 11.00am-2.30pm, 6.00pm-11.00pm

Beers: Courage - Best Bitter
            Hook Norton - Old Hook
            Wadsworth - 6X

Terrain

Open fields and heathland with no steep climbs. Most of the paths are
well walked so waymarking tends to be good.

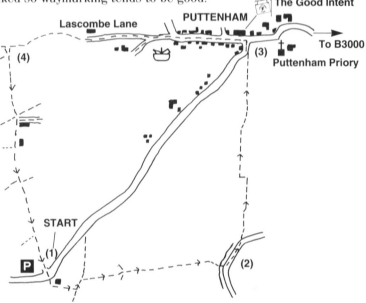

Getting to the Start (Grid Ref. 921461)

The walk starts from the Puttenham Common car park, which is
signposted as well as being marked on the Ordnance Survey Map. To
get there make your way to Puttenham village and take the road
opposite The Good Intent pub. After approximately 1¼ miles the lane
bends sharp right in front of a cottage, and the entrance to the car
park, which is signposted, is on your right. Alternatively, take the
B3001, and just to the west of Elstead, take a road signposted to
Puttenham. Go straight on at a crossroads, passing Cutt Mill Ponds
and continue until the lane bends sharp left in front of a cottage and
you will see the car park on your left.

The Walk

(1) From the car park walk down the track on which you entered by
car. Cross the road and at the other side pass to the right of the
cottage to take a signposted footpath. After descending onto a
sunken path turn left, then after fifteen paces turn right onto

another path. On meeting a junction of paths continue straight ahead in the direction of a yellow arrow, following a fence on your right. This leads you to a field where you should continue straight ahead going downhill and keeping to the edge of the field. At the far side of the field maintain your route ahead along a grass track and over a succession of stiles to shortly arrive at a lane.

¼ mile **(2)** Turn left along the lane and after about 75 metres take a signposted Public Footpath left to enter a field. Keep to the left hand edge of the field to reach a stile at the far side, which you should cross to enter another field. Go diagonally right across the centre of the next field and after going over a stile into a third field, turn left to follow the perimeter round. At the far corner of the field go over two stiles in quick succession and follow a fenced path to arrive at an open field beside a derelict pergola. The large house ahead to your right is Puttenham Priory, a fine paladin mansion. Maintain your route ahead by following a grass track along the edge of the field and at the far side, on meeting a lane, continue straight on to reach a "T" junction at the centre of Puttenham village.

Centuries ago Puttenham is said to have welcomed pilgrims on their way from Winchester to the shrine of Thomas a Becket at Canterbury. At the eastern end of the village is the church which is of Norman origin. Its squat tower used to support a spire which was destroyed by fire in 1735.

¼ miles **(3)** Turn left at the "T" junction past the front of the pub and follow the road through the village until it bends right beside the Pilgrim's News newsagent. Leave the road at this point and follow Lascombe Lane ahead. After a short distance fork right and follow the lane to its end where you should continue ahead along a path marked by a red arrow and a white acorn. Keep to the path until it forks in front of a Surrey County Council information sign for Puttenham Common.

¼ miles **(4)** Take the path to the left of the sign and after approximately 20 metres turn left onto a prominent crossing path. Keep to the path ignoring all turnings off to eventually come out at a small parking area beside a pretty cottage on your left. Continue straight ahead here along a track, to shortly after pass a large white house on your left. From here maintain your route along the track ignoring any further turnings off, and continue until you see a green and picnic tables with the car park on your right. Cross the green back

¼ miles to the car park, our starting point.

The Merry Harriers
- Hambledon

Free House. Outside hangs a sign stating "Open For Warm Beer And Lousy Food", and of course, the opposite is true. Step inside this 16th century hostelry and you will discover one of Surrey's least spoilt pubs, serving some of the best kept beer in the county. The pub's large shaggy dog (as much part of the pub as the furniture) greets you as you enter the front bar. The bar itself has many original features, including a lovely inglenook fire and from the beamed ceiling hangs a collection of chamber pots. To the left is a pool room, whilst the bar extends round to the right, with a picture of the pub dog on the wall and with the chamber pots changing to a jumble of old bottles, brass and utensils from the past. Outside is a large beer garden and opposite, the pub runs a small campsite. There is a good bar food menu which will keep you going for the second half of the walk. The pub is bound to make an impression, let's hope in this world of change that The Merry Harriers continues to resist it.

 *(Campsite)* . *11.00am-3.00pm, 6.00pm-11.00pm*

Beers: Friary Meux - Best Bitter
                Ind Coope - Burton Ale
                Youngs - Special

Terrain

Undulating farm and woodland. Most of the paths are well walked so route finding is fairly easy. In one or two places and especially along the path approaching the pub the going can get very muddy.

Getting to the Start (Grid Ref. 979402)

The walk starts from the National Trust car park for Hydon's Ball at Hydon Heath and is marked on the Ordnance Survey Map. The easiest way to get there is from Milford (south of Godalming), take the road that is signposted to Milford Railway Station. Follow this until you reach a crossroads, and go straight on to follow Salt Lane signposted to Dunsfold and Hascombe. The car park is approximately 3/4 mile along this road opposite a turning left, signposted to Goldalming, the car park is then up a track signposted only by a National Trust sign for Hydon's Ball. After about 50 metres you turn left into the car park itself. Please note, the car park is quite hard to find so pay careful attention to the directions. The pub is easier to find as it is signposted from the A283 as 'warm beer and lousy food'.

The Walk

(1) To start the walk, from the car park walk back along the track to Salt Lane and just before you meet it take a signposted Public Bridleway left. The bridleway runs along the perimeter of the wood and then joins a wider path coming in from the left. Here you should carry straight on, keeping to the main path at all times which is also marked by blue arrows on short wooden stumps. Do not be tempted to turn off. Eventually the path arrives at a crossing path, also marked by blue arrows and here you should maintain your route continuing straight on. You will soon go over another crossing path after which the path runs along a fence on your left (this could disappear in the future). Eventually the path descends and leaves the wood to run between fields before arriving at a road in front of a house.

¾ mile   **(2)** Cross the road and follow a track the other side, signposted as a Public Bridleway. Do not enter the car park but keep to the track to later pass a couple of cottages and then pass to the left of a barn, continuing straight on to now cross a golf course. The track crosses a green and then runs through a strip of woodland, before crossing a second green. At the end of the second green on meeting another strip of woodland turn left, thereby leaving the track and following the edge of the green with the wood on your right. You should now find yourself going uphill and after about 50 metres should bear right to follow a prominent path through the wood. The path runs along the top of a wooded cliff and in Winter when the trees are bare you have good views of a stream below. The path descends to cross the stream via a wooden bridge, after which you should turn left and follow the path alongside a lone property before passing through some wooden rails into a field.

(3) Bear left to follow the edge of the field, later passing a pond, after which you should maintain your route. Leave the field at the far side, passing through a gate into a wood. Fork left beside some electricity poles in the direction of the yellow footpath arrow and at a crossing path marked by a set of yellow arrows turn left. Keep to the main path going over a number of crossing paths, to shortly arrive at a "T" junction marked by a wooden post and some blue arrows. Turn left to follow a path that soon bends right, leaving the wood to run between fields, eventually arriving at a lane beside The Merry Harriers pub.

1½ miles

(4) Take a signposted Public Footpath opposite the pub and follow this

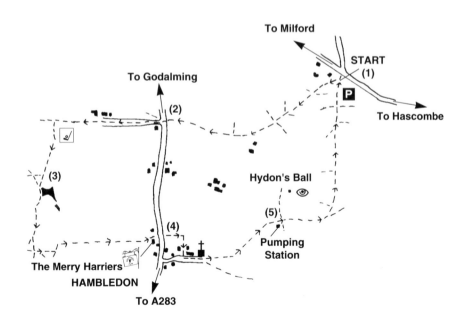

uphill to arrive at a driveway running between cottages. Follow the drive and then turn left along a lane to arrive at St. Peter's church. In the churchyard is a hollow yew and legend has it that if you walk round the tree three times a witch will appear. Keep to the lane and pass to the right of the church, fork left at the turning area, following the churchyard wall passing an ancient lime kiln before entering a field. Cross the field and at the far side, pass through a kissing gate and bear diagonally left across the next field heading for the far left hand corner. On reaching the corner leave the field and follow a narrow path ahead which almost immediately bends right to pass through a sweet chestnut coppice.

(5) At a junction beside the Thames Water Hydon Ball Sub Station continue ahead now following a wide track. (A short detour taking a path left here with take you to the top of Hydon's Ball where there is a monument and glorious views of the surrounding countryside.) The track gradually bears round to the left and to avoid getting lost you should keep to it at all times ignoring any turnings off, including marked bridleways. Eventually the track will lead you back to the car park, our starting point.

Nearby Attractions
Winkworth Arboretum N.T. Hillside of many rare trees and shrubs overlooking two lakes. There is a tea room and shop at the entrance.
Witley Common N.T. Extensive pine woods with a visitors and information centre.

Ordnance Survey Landranger Map 187

King William IV
- Mickleham

Free House. Set in the side of White Hill this lovely pub was once an alehouse for the staff of Lord Beaverbrook's estate. The pub has two bars and a terraced garden. Being on the side of a steep hill, all are reached by a series of steps which must be negotiated with care if you intend sampling all of the excellent beers on offer. The main bar has a real fire and is furnished in the traditional style. The smaller bar is marked 'private' and has room for just two people at the bar and a couple of tables. It still has it's original "planked" walls and is very cosy, especially in Winter. The garden offers lovely views across the Mole Gap and is popular with walkers. The proprietor is also the chef, the reason why the food is so good and why people visit from miles around. To be certain of getting a table in the evening it is wise to book ahead. The menu is carefully selected with a good choice of vegetarian dishes. A traditional roast is served every Sunday and, in Summer, a barbecue is often held in the garden. Please note, food is not available on Monday evenings and the menu is reduced on Bank Holidays and Sundays.

 *11.00am-3.00pm, 6.00pm-11.00pm*

Beers: Adnams - Southwold Bitter
                Badger - Best Bitter
                Boddingtons - Bitter
                Hogs Back - T.E.A., Rip Snorter (Winter only)

Terrain

Tracks (often very muddy) and well marked paths through open scrub and woodland. The descent and climb of White Hill to the pub is quite steep and care is needed.

Getting to the Start (Grid Ref. 193546)

The walk starts from a small parking area opposite Nower Wood (marked) and west of Headley on the B2033. From the west, the B2033 is reached from the A24 just outside Leatherhead and is signposted to Headley. The road soon passes between Tyrrels Wood Golf Course and when this ends, the parking area is on the right, just after the entrance to a car park for Nower Wood Nature Reserve on the left. From the east, the B2033 is reached via the B2032 which connects the A25 with the A217, the B2033 is signposted to Leatherhead. After passing Headley cricket pitch, turn left still following the signs for Leatherhead, and follow the road through the outskirts of Headley and then between fields. Just as you reach some woodland you will see the parking area on your left.

The Walk

(1) From the parking area, take the track (bridleway) which forks right that soon follows the edge of Tyrrels Wood Golf Course. Follow the bridleway for approximately 3/4 of a mile until it joins a wide track where there is a gate on your left and another track off to the right. Continue ahead along the track for a further 25 paces and turn left onto a wide path, marked with a red arrow. This goes downhill and passes a large house on your right, after which it continues in a straight line through Cherkley Wood, devastated in the storm of 1987. Keep to the path until it forks in front of a National Trust sign for Mickleham Downs where you should fork right.

1¼ miles   **(2)** Continue for some distance until you meet a marked crossing path where you should turn right in the direction of a blue arrow. A few paces after, you will reach another crossing path and a stile on your right. Carry straight on here along a narrow path which winds through woodland, at one point passing a wooden post marking the route of a National Trust Long Walk. Soon after, the path begins to descend the side of Mickleham Downs, where there are lovely views ahead across the Mole Gap to Norbury Park. The descent is quite steep in places, so take care. Near the bottom of the hill, go over a wide crossing path and continue downhill to soon arrive at the King William IV pub.

(3) After passing in front of the pub, turn left along a lane and after a few paces (before you reach the A24), turn left along another lane. Pass St. Michael's School, immediately after which you should fork right to follow a track ahead which soon ends in front of a recreation ground. Fork right again here, and follow a narrow path past Lammas Cottage. When the path meets a "T" junction, turn left along another path. Go over a lane and continue following a path ahead and on reaching the graveyard to Mickleham church, if you want to visit The Running Horses pub, turn right. If not, carry straight on through the churchyard and at the other side, turn left along a gravel drive. (N.B. If you have decided to stop at The Running Horses, then you will have to retrace your steps to continue the walk).

1¾ miles

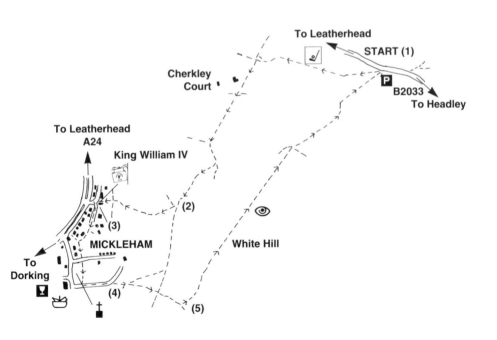

2¼ miles **(4)** When the drive meets a white gate, go over a stile to your right and follow a narrow path up the steep side of Mickleham Downs. At a fork, take the righthand path and, as you near the top of the hill, go over a wide crossing track and continue following a narrow path ahead. When this meets a National Trust post marked with the number "6" and with two blue Long Walk arrows, fork left in the direction of the arrow to follow a narrow path through the wood along the top of the hill. (N.B. If you find yourself starting to descend, then you will have missed the fork left).

2½ miles **(5)** When the path reaches the grass summit of White Hill, bear right to follow the wide grass track along the top of the hill, in the direction of a National Trust Long Walk arrow. On reaching the far side of the grass hilltop, pass under a wire fence to now follow a well used track ahead. This time, take no notice of the National Trust Long Walk arrow which after a few paces points right. Keep to the track 4 miles and follow it ahead back to the car park, our starting point.

Nearby Attractions

Box Hill N.T. A famous hill with glorious views to the South Downs.

Denbies Vineyard. The largest vineyard in England, complete with visitors centre.

Chapel Farm - West Humble. A farm open to the public offering trailer rides, fun for children.

Polesden Lacey N.T. Fine 1820's Regency villa where King George VI and Queen Elizabeth, the Queen Mother, spent part of their honeymoon.

Ordnance Survey Landranger Map 187

Stephan Langton
- Friday Street

Free House. One of the most secluded pubs in Surrey, the Stephan Langton is well worth searching out. It has an idyllic setting in a tiny hamlet with a hammer pond and surrounded by steep wooded valley sides. Inside the pub has a very cosy feel with a carpeted bar and in Winter a real fire. There is a separate restaurant as well as bar food. All the meals are home cooked and the pub specialises in local produce such as game or trout. The menu also includes a good selection of deserts for those with a sweet tooth. The pub does not have a garden, but there are a number of tables at the front and on a narrow terrace at the back which overlooks a small stream.

✗ iOi ⼤ . **OPEN** *11.00am-2.30pm, 6.00pm-11.00pm*

Beers: Bass - Bitter
               Fullers - London Pride
               Youngs - Special

Terrain

Mainly woodland paths crossing and following a number of streams. Although the route is up and down, there is nothing too strenuous.

Getting to the Start (Grid Ref. 126457)

The walk starts from the public car park at Friday Street. To get there from the A25 west of Wotton, or the B2126, follow the signs to Friday Street. The car park is well signposted. Please do not attempt to park at the pub as there is only room for a small number of cars and the public car park is only a few minutes walk away.

The Walk

(1) To start, from the car park facing the road walk to the right hand corner of the car park then follow a path downhill which runs parallel with the road. After going down some steps join the road and continue downhill to meet the pond at Friday Street. Turn left onto a track signposted as a Public Footpath, passing to the left of Pond Cottage. Keep to the track, at one point crossing a stream via a rickety wooden bridge. Later, fork left past Yew Tree Cottage and continue until you meet a gate with a stone bridge on your left.

¼ mile (2) Turn right here to go over a stile and follow a fenced path uphill. As the path levels out it bends right and widens to become more of a track. Stay on it as it later bends left and when it bends left again, leave it to take a path on your right. To ensure you have taken the right path, you should have a field on your right and woodland on your left. Keep to the path which runs alongside the field to meet and cross a lane. Continue ahead following a fenced path and when the fencing ends, maintain your route, now going downhill. Near the bottom follow the path left to enter a field. Take a prominent grass path across the centre of the field to shortly cross the Tillingbourne river and continue to go over a stile at the far side of the field onto a track.

¾ mile (3) Turn right and follow the track passing to the right of a house and later a splendid waterfall. Afterwards the track bends right taking you over the Tillingbourne once more before eventually ending at a lane in front of Triple Bar Riding Centre. Turn left along the lane, ignoring a signposted bridleway on the left to pass through the hamlet of Broadmoor. When the lane ends beside Whiteberry Cottage, continue ahead along a wide path which follows a line of telegraph poles.

2 miles (4) Eventually the path bends left to meet a track onto which you should turn right. After approximately 50 metres the track bends sharp right, turning back on itself and you should leave it at this point to follow a wide path ahead. Stay on the path until you arrive at a junction of tracks. To ensure you have the right spot you will see a gate on your left marked as a footpath with a dragon carved on the gatepost. Turn right at this point and follow the track, almost going back on yourself, later ignoring a turning off to the left to reach a lane.

(5) Cross the lane and take the signposted Public Footpath the other side which, after winding through a wood, leads out to a field. Go straight across the field aiming just right of the house visible ahead, and then follow a hedged path which runs alongside the garden to the house. After passing a second house, the path once more enters woodland and descends into a valley to meet a crossing track.

2½ miles

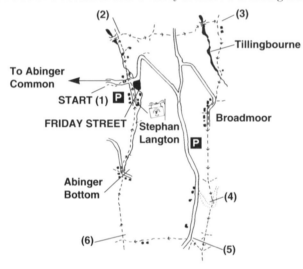

(6) Turn right onto the crossing track and follow it gently downhill to eventually arrive at a pretty hamlet known as Hammer Bottom. On reaching a lane, proceed to follow it ahead and after about 30 metres leave it to join a wide path on your right. Pass a pretty wooden bridge, maintaining your route downhill, following a stream on your right to eventually reach the first houses of Friday Street. A short distance along a tarmac lane brings you to the Stephan Langton pub. *Friday Street was once a hamlet at the heart of the iron industry. The pond known as a hammer pond was created to supply water to drive a giant hammer which would crush the iron ore. The pub is named after the Archbishop of Canterbury who held office during the reign of King John. Archbishop Langton was born at Friday Street in 1150.* After the pub, follow the lane to soon reach the hammer pond and turn left to retrace your steps back to the car park, our starting point.

3 miles

4 miles

Nearby Attractions

Leith Hill N.T. The highest hill in the south east of England, complete with viewing tower.

Wotton Church - Wotton. A beautiful 13th century church where the diarist John Evelyn is buried. Above the entrance door are eight carved heads, one is said to be the earliest carving of a Pope to be found in England.

The Blue Bell Inn
- Dockenfield

*Free House. This lovely isolated 16th century pub was once the village
bakery. Inside a number of small rooms lead off the tiny main bar.
Some of the rooms are only opened when the pub gets busy. The main
bar has painted brick walls with a large fireplace, the original fire
being replaced by one of those clever gas imitations. There is a
separate lounge (without a bar) which has a number of interesting
pieces of furniture. The many windows in this room make it a delight
in which to relax in Summer. Outside there is a large garden with
swings and a treehouse and in Summer, a beautiful display of 'cottage
garden' flowers. Food comes in the form of simple bar meals which
include excellent home-made soup. Beers are served direct from the
cask which is stored behind the bar.*

 , ⍭ , *6.00pm - 11.00pm*

(temporarily closed weekday lunchtimes)

Weekends 11.00am - 3.00pm, 6.00pm - 11.00pm.

Beers: Adnams - Southwold Bitter
Ballards - Best Bitter

Terrain

Gentle rolling hills and river valleys. Most of the paths are well walked with those near water becoming very muddy in wet weather.

Getting to the Start (Grid Ref. 844405)

The walk starts at the main car park for Frensham Great Pond. To get there take the A287 to Lane End which is between Millbridge and Churt and from there take the road beside a small green, signposted to Frensham Common as well as Headley. It is only a short distance along the road to the car park which is well signposted.

The Walk

(1) From the car park walk down to the edge of Frensham Great Pond then turn right and follow a broad path along the edge of the pond. *The pond is fed by a natural spring and in the early 13th century was used to provide the Bishop of Winchester with fresh fish. In 1913, the pond was used in tests for the very first sea-plane.* Keeping to the edge of the pond you will eventually come out at a lane onto which you should turn left. After about 50 metres and just before the lane goes over a small bridge, turn right onto a signposted Public Bridleway. You will soon pass a pond after which you should maintain your route, keeping to the higher path. After a short distance the path meets and follows the course of the River Wey (do not turn off) to eventually, after passing through the courtyard to "The Mill House", come out at a lane. Turn left along the lane, skirting the millpond and going over the mill race to shortly arrive at a "T" junction. Cross the road ahead and turn left to walk along the grass verge the other side.

(2) Just before you reach a pair of cottages, turn right onto a signposted Public Bridleway and follow this between fields. The farm with the oasthouses on your right is an indication that this was once a famous hop growing area. The bridleway eventually leads out to a lane. Turn right and follow the lane past some pretty cottages and when the lane ends continue ahead along a signposted Public Bridleway. On meeting a tarmac drive, bear left and follow the drive to soon arrive at The Blue Bell Inn. *1¼ miles*

(3) From the inn turn right and follow the lane that runs past the pub car park and on meeting a road turn right, then immediately right again onto a track which is signposted as leading to Batts Corner Kennels. After about 50 metres go over a stile on your right, then *2¼ miles*

turn left and follow the edge of a field. Go over a stile into a second field and maintain your route passing to the right of the kennels. On reaching the field corner go over another stile to now follow a prominent path through a wood. Do not be tempted to turn off but keep to the path which gradually widens to become a track. Keep to the track ignoring all turnings off to eventually leave the wood and follow the righthand edge of a field. You are now also running along the spine of a hill which affords lovely views to both your left and right.

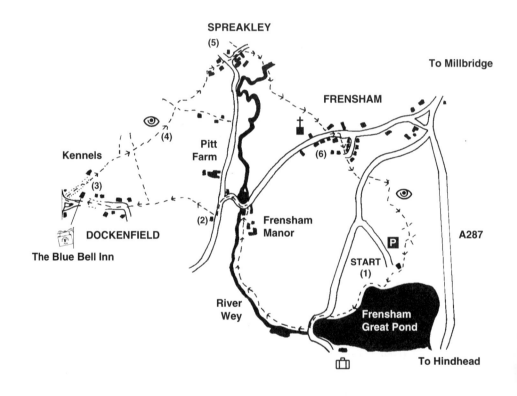

3 miles **(4)** When the track bends left at the far side of the field, leave it to follow a narrow path ahead, once again through woodland. Follow the path downhill through the wood to a stile. Go over the stile,

turn left and follow the edge of a field. After about 50 metres as the field perimeter begins to bend right, go left into a small grass clearing and go over a stile ahead, this is the second stile on the left. This takes you once again into woodland and you should follow a narrow but well established path ahead. On entering another field maintain your route ahead along the field edge and after passing a large house on your right, go over a stile on the same side, then through a small gate to follow a narrow path ahead which runs parallel with the drive to the house. The path soon joins the drive and you should bear left to follow the drive down to a road.

(5) Cross the road to follow another road ahead marked as a dead end, then after about 50 metres take the Public Footpath on your right. This is tarmacced and leads downhill to cross the River Wey. Soon after crossing the river turn left along a tarmac drive and follow this to arrive at Frensham village beside the church. *Inside the church is a large copper cauldron which, it is claimed, belonged to Mother Ludlam, the Waverley Witch. There are also stories that it came from the kitchen of Waverley Abbey, though its most likely use was for church ales in the Middle Ages.* 3½ miles

(6) Cross the road and turn left, then right onto a Public Footpath beside 'The Toll House'. Follow the path to shortly cross a small residential road and maintain your route following the path the other side to eventually reach another road. Turn left along the road, then after a few paces, right onto a signposted Public Footpath. The path leads up the side of a hill where at the top you are rewarded with fine views over Frensham Great Pond. Turn right and take the wide path that runs along the top of the hill and follow it as it bends left to descend the other side. At the bottom go over a wide crossing path evidently used a lot by horses and follow a narrow path ahead marked by a low wooden sign 'No Horses No Cycles'. At the next crossing path turn right and follow it without turning off to soon arrive back at the car park, our starting point. 4 miles

4½ miles

Nearby Attractions
Alice Holt Forest. Large forest managed by The Forestry Commission. There is a good visitors centre and nature trail.
Bird World. Privately run bird park, famous for its collection of parrots.

The Plough - Coldharbour

Free House. At 850 ft. above sea level The Plough is the highest pub in the south-east of England. Because of its remote position it has preserved its own distinct character and is all the better for it. The rustic front bar gives way to a small restaurant on the right which has a real fire in a fireplace made from local stone. There are guns displayed above the bar, a reminder that until recently hunting here was a way of life. Above the fireplace hangs a cricket bat and a sign telling patrons that The Plough is the home to Coldharbour Cricket Club who play on the highest cricket ground in the south-east. A separate bar to the rear has a pool table and generally acts as a games area. If you are a beer lover, then you are in for a treat, for The Plough offers no less than ten real ales and even real cider. The menu is also extensive and serves some hearty meals, as one would expect in walking country. I am sure you will agree that The Plough is hard to beat and worth more than a short visit. One answer is to take advantage of their bed and breakfast. The rooms have glorious views and Anna's traditional breakfast has to be seen to be believed.

11.00am-3.00pm, 6.00pm-11.00pm

Beers: Adnams - Broadside
Gibbs Mew - Bishops Tipple
Badger - Best Bitter, Tanglefoot
Pilgrims - Talisman
Ringwood - Old Thumper
Theakston - Old Peculier
Guest Beers
Cider: Biddenden - Kentish Cider

Terrain

Nearly all woodland paths and tracks. Some steep gradients and long steady climbs which can be very tiring. Much of the route can also get quite muddy.

Getting to the Start (Grid Ref. 131432)

The walk starts from Starveall Corner Car Park on the side of Leith Hill. There are many ways to get to the car park, but unless you have local knowledge, the easiest way is from the A25. Leave the A25 just west of Wotton to follow a road north signposted to Abinger Common, Friday Street and Leith Hill. Keep to the road following the signs for Coldharbour and after approximately 3 miles you will see the car park (which is signposted) on your left.

The Walk

(1) From the car park walk behind the information sign and go over a wooden bridge to follow a path signposted to the Tower. After a few paces you will meet a crossing path and another path joining from the left. Turn left onto the crossing path and follow this in a straight line through woodland. Ignore all turnings off including a prominent crossing path but keep to the main path eventually descending to arrive at a "T" junction. As a guide this is approximately ¾ of a mile from where we began at the car park.

The extensive woodland through which we pass was once a haven for smugglers and no doubt some of the paths we follow originated from their activities. Locally, many of the paths are still known as silk and brandy trails, the smugglers main booty. The woodland was the perfect hiding place for smuggling contraband. To be especially sure their booty was safe from detection, the smugglers would bury it. Occasionally a local would stumble across such a hide and, if this happened, he would mark certain items with a white cross and return them to the lair. The smuggler would then leave the marked items as a token of thanks for the silence of the finder.

¾ miles **(2)** Turn right at the "T" junction along a track to after approximately 50 metres arrive at a crossing track. As a guide ahead of you is a one bar gate with a dragon on the righthand gate post. Turn left and follow a wide path downhill, ignoring all turnings off, to eventually arrive at a gravel drive on a horseshoe bend. Join the drive on the righthand side of the horseshoe and follow it for approximately 50 metres when you should take a well used path on the left, continuing your route downhill. Once again, ignore any turnings off to eventually arrive at a tarmac lane at the hamlet of Broadmoor.

1¼ miles **(3)** Maintain your route along the lane passing a number of pretty cottages and when the lane bends left beside Triple Bar Riding Centre, take the first turning right, a track signposted as a bridleway and also as a private road. Keep to the track (do not turn off) and when it forks beside Pond Cottage maintain your route ahead by taking the righthand track.

1¾ miles **(4)** The track eventually forks again and this time you should take the lefthand track to shortly pass behind the beautiful Warren Farm. After the farm go over the Tillingbourne where you will see a pond on your left, fed by a series of mini waterfalls which come from Tilling Springs, the source of the Tillingbourne. When the track bends left to service a house, leave it to join a marked bridleway ahead, now entering an area known as Dukes Warren. After a short distance leave the track to take an unmarked, fairly prominent path on your left leading uphill. After about 20 metres this leads to another wider path onto which you should turn left. The path runs along the side of a valley and when it forks you should take the righthand fork to continue your route up the side of the valley. Go over a crossing track and follow another track ahead which soon narrows to become a path and later runs alongside a field on your left before meeting a wide track onto which you should turn right.

2¾ miles **(5)** You must now stay on the track ignoring all turnings off to eventually join another track where there is a Forestry Commission sign asking you to protect wildlife by keeping dogs on a lead. Maintain your route ahead and the track will lead you to Coldharbour and The Plough, the highest pub in south-east England.

3 miles **(6)** From the track where you entered Coldharbour, turn right passing between a post box and telephone box to follow another track uphill at first passing some cottages. When the track forks take the righthand fork, passing to the right of an emergency access

sign and thereafter keep to the track to later pass the highest cricket pitch in the south-east of England. The track forks beside the cricket pitch and here you should take the lefthand fork to pass (do not take) a path on your left marked with a green arrow. Later the track meets and follows an ancient stone wall on your right. In places this has become somewhat overgrown with moss and grass and can easily be mistaken for a bank. Keep to the main

track ignoring all turnings off until it eventually forks, taking the righthand fork, the less prominent track downhill still following the wall (bank) on your right. If you miss this turning, simply turn right at the next junction of tracks where there is a one bar gate on your left and a green topped post on your right. Both tracks end up at the same place. At the next junction of tracks take the track which leads uphill in the direction of the sign for the Tower. This is the last climb of the walk and leads to the top of Leith Hill, the highest point in the south-east of England which is crowned by a tower. At weekends you can get light refreshments here.

Leith Hill is 965 ft high and the Tower brings the total height of the hill to 1,000 ft. The Tower was built in 1776 by Richard Hull whose body was later found bricked up inside, this having been his dying wish. When the Tower is open, for a small fee you can climb to the top where on a clear day you are said to be able to see parts of thirteen counties.

4 miles **(7)** Pass the front of the tower and take the main track ahead which is shortly signposted to Starveall Corner Car Park. Keep to the main track, do not turn off until you see a prominent path leading right, which is marked with the shape of a car with an 'S' in the middle. Take this and follow the path back to Starvealls Corner Car Park, 5 miles our starting point.

Nearby Attractions
Denbies Vineyard - Dorking. The largest vineyard in England with a visitors centre and shop.
Box Hill N.T. Prominent hill on the North Downs, famous for its views.